CW00515236

As You
There's
at the T
and The
Where That Came From Because...

# I'll Show You How to Discover the HIDDEN WEALTH in Your Dental Practice Absolutely FREE – if You ACT NOW!

Dear Friend,

No matter how hard you work you just can't seem to get ahead -- or give your family the things dentists' families enjoyed when you were a kid.

You know why -- managed care, patients who refuse needed treatment, staff hassles -- all the things that leave you driving to work every day with stress as your passenger. Which is why t's so important that you read this letter, and learn how you can:

### Totally Obliterate the Things That Are Killing Your Practice and Double...Even Triple Your Income

You know me. I'm Dr. Tom Orent. You've read my columns, maybe even bought my books or attended my seminars.

People call me "the Gems Guy" because my easy-to-implement practice and income-building ideas (GEMS!) have changed the lives of 16,543 dentists for the better.

> My life feels forever changed as we have been averaging almost an **extra $50,000** in production, above and beyond what was once normal'". -- *Dr. Kory Wegner, Milwaukee, WI*

My gems were born out of necessity. My practice had one foot in the grave I needed strategies that were quick and effective (not to mention cheap). And I discovered a ton of them, with the result that in just three years I went from the brink of financial ruin to being richer than I ever dreamed.

> Who would have imagined that easy-to-follow instructions and simple ideas like the ones I chose to act on from Tom's monthly communications would do this: **in 4 short months I doubled my income!**
> *Dr. Chris Bowman, Charlotte, NC*

All the things I did work for you? Check out what dentists across the country and beyond are saying. Then, if you're ready for success at warp speed, reach out and

help yourself to **five months worth of:**

## Gems Insiders' Circle Silver Membership FREE.
### NO RISK. NO CHARGE. NO STRINGS. NO HYPE.

You'll get a giant cache of gems, including three recent months of materials plus two months going forward, all for a one-time charge of $5.95 to cover postage.

Your **Fully Guaranteed**, trial membership includes:

- Three recent, strategy-crammed issues of my *Independent Dentist Newsletter* as soon as you sign up followed by an exciting new issue every month. This brainstorm-filled publication is THE resource for dentists who ready to get in on the action.
- Instant access to my *Million Dollar Resources Directory,* the place to find everything you need cheap -- or at least at the very best prices.
- Three of my most recent *"Mastermind of the Month"* CD series -- interviews with Masterminds like Dr. Gordon Christensen, Dr. Charles Blair, Mr. Greg Stanley, Dr. Ray Bertolotti and many others you may have not had the opportunity to hear. You'll also receive additional Mastermind CDs delivered monthly -- PLUS 15 AGD-PACE credits per year just for listening to (and profiting from) them.
- *Breakthrough thinking from the archives of Mr. Alan Thornberg*, practice transition specialist and all-around genius.
- *Five Silver Letter* inserts (three recent, two ongoing.) These monthly communications from the edge bristle with unorthodox, but highly effective ideas.

> "Since we began receiving your gems, just 9 months ago, our collectible production is up **over $116,000 a year** and most of that increase is NET PROFIT! "-- *Carter Gampp, DDS, Phoenix, AZ*

### Are You Starting to See How Much This Could Mean to You?
Read on -- and keep in mind I'm just

scratching the surface of all you'll receive.

- *Three recent issues of my GoldMine Newsletter:* Lots of dentists consider this monthly publication absolutely essential to their success.
- Twice a year my Silver members receive a CD with studio quality photos of great new VIP patient gifts and information on where you can buy them wholesale -- often at savings of 40 - 60%. As a FREE TRIAL Member you'll receive one of these CDs, too, with JPEG images, you can drop them into ads, flyers, postcards -- whatever you need to impress entice and motivate your best patients.
- *Private e-mail access to me* through members' "Ask The Gems Guy"!
- The chance to sit in on live quarterly *teleconferences with my masterminds.*

> "I have **doubled my income** in the last five months and have had time to take several weeks off."
> -- *Ranvir Dhillon, DMD, Hounslow, England*

### Access Online 24/7 to Gems Proprietary Strategic Documents
Take a look at just some of what you'll find waiting for you:

- **"The Secret to How I Resigned From Delta But KEPT Most of My Delta Patients!"**
- **"Seven Magic Phrases Your Dental Receptionist Can Use Today** to Effortlessly Build an IRON CAGE Around Your Patients... Case 'Acceptance' is NOT 'Acceptance' until you INSURE Acceptance of Your Financial Arrangements."
- **"A Financial Options Form to Help Patients Say Yes While Making YOU a TON More Money"**
- **"VERBAL SKILLS that NAIL 87% Adult Acceptance of Fluoride."**
- "Discover the Secret to **Effortlessly & Instantly Boosting Your Average Cosmetic Case Acceptance**

# OFFER ENDS
# 10 DAYS FROM BOOK SHIP DATE

## FOR *FASTEST* ACTION FAX NOW TO 1-508-861-1550

❑ YES, <u>PLEASE SIGN ME UP</u>
**for the GIC FREE TRIAL SILVER MEMBERSHIP.**
I authorize you to bill my credit card $5.95 now and $79.50 per month starting in Month 3. **I AM FREE TO CANCEL AT ANY TIME and keep everything I've received.**

*For your protection, **<u>please include the 3-digit Security Code</u>** on the back of your card.*

Doctor's Name _____

Address _____

City_____State_____Zip_____Country _____

Phone_____Fax _____

Email _____

**Credit Card:**
❑ MC     ❑ Visa  ❑ Amex     ❑ Disc     Expiration Date____/_____

Card # _____3-digit code _____

Exact Name on Card: _____

**Cardholder Signature:** _____

My signature here authorizes Dr. Tom Orent and Gems Publishing USA, Inc. to charge the credit card listed for the amounts shown, and to use email, fax, phone and mailing addresses to keep me informed of new products and special offers made available from time to time.

ECSBK-2

# Extreme
# Customer
# Service

## Beyond the Edge

Dr. Tom Orent

# Extreme Customer Service
## Beyond the Edge

by Dr. Tom Orent

First Edition - Copyright © 1999 Gems Publishing

ISBN 0-9651544-2-4

Edited by Lynn R. Berman
Cartoon illustrations by Rich Parsons

**Cover**:
Photography and graphics by Roberto Gaseta
Filmed on location at REI, Framingham, MA
Technical assistance, on belay, Josh Connell


Published by:
**Gems Publishing** ™
12 Walnut Street
Framingham, MA 01702

To Brendon, Shayna and Alexandra
My incredibly
wonderful children

# TABLE OF CONTENTS

INTRODUCTION                                    9

I'LL MEET YOU AT THE MALL                      16

MARY AND ALI                                   25

THE "ORGANIZATION" ORGANIZATION                29

ABOUT YOUR PHONE                               34

LEXUS!                                         39

PASS IT ON. *PLEASE!*                          41

PERSONAL TOUCH                                 44

FORESIGHT = *WOW*                              46

A STANDARD LET-DOWN                            48

SMALL PHONE, *EXTREME* SERVICE                 51

SHUTTLE DIPLOMACY                              54

THE ANSWER IS *YES!* 57

A MATTER OF POLICY (*YOU LOSE*) 60

THE *EXTREME* ISP 66

THE SPA 68

MAY I *PLEASE* USE YOUR PHONE? 71

SPORTS TALK RADIO 74

WE LISTEN. BUT DO WE *REALLY* HEAR? 77

WHAT'S *YOUR* NAME? 79

WHAT TIME DO *YOU* CLOSE? 83

WHAT TIME DO *WE* CLOSE? 91

THRIFTY ANGEL 95

THE BUS 96

LATE FOR THEIR MEETINGS 101

MONDAY, BY 6:00 P.M.! 103

STAPLES. AND *MUCH* MORE. 105

IT'S *ONLY* NINETY CENTS 109

6

PASS ON THE POWER 114

DADDY, ARE *WE* HOMELESS? 116

THE CAB 122

THE *EXTREME* DREAM 124

Part I: At the Restaurant 125

Part II: The Airlines 130

Part III: Technical Support 134

Part IV: The Gas Station 142

*EXTREME* CONSISTENCY 144

IN THE LAND OF THE *BLINDS* 145

SATISFACTION *GUARANTEED* 148

THE "BRIDE" 149

FAR AWAY FROM HOME 151

*EXTREME* PERSONAL 152

*BEYOND* THE *JOB* DESCRIPTION 154

"GUARANTEED" LATE RESERVATION 156

A *THIRST* FOR CUSTOMER SERVICE 158

THE CLOTHES *MAKE* THE MAN            160

CHEF JEFF                            162

L'ESPALIER                           167

MAINTAINING *SIGHT* OF CUSTOMER
SERVICE                              169

*INFINITI* CUSTOMER SERVICE!         171

*SOLE* OF THE ORGANIZATION           173

*SENSITIVITY* TO SENSITIVITY         177

HOW THE "WILD ONES" GOT THEIR NAME179

SWEAT THE *SMALL* STUFF              186

VIP *ONE*-STAR CUSTOMER SERVICE!     188

FOUR SEASONS.                        192

*FIVE STARS.*                        192

*PRE*-MANAGING EXPECTATIONS          195

FINE, IS NOT                         202

CONCLUSION                           206

"In the land of the blind,

the one-eyed man is king."

– Anonymous

## Introduction

They are two *extreme* **opposite ends of the universe**: great customer service... and the *horror* stories we hear all too often. Extreme Customer Service explores *both* ends. Odds are, you're probably somewhere in the middle. **You're in a very dangerous place** – realize it or not.

Why did Tom Peters say that *Kaizen* (the Japanese management theory of continuous incremental improvement, popular in the 1980s) is "far too little, too late?" Drucker uses words like, "Abandon everything!" In a 1997 lecture, Peters lauded Bill Gates' 180-degree shift aiming Microsoft headfirst into the Internet. Peters called it **one of the boldest moves in the history of the computer industry**: either Gates would take the company down in flames, *or* he'd be the first computer giant to maintain a position of dominance beyond a single decade!

Before you read any further, consider **Dr. Stephen Covey warning** *against* **retooling your customer service focus:**you could become the worlds' leading example of five-star customer service, yet *still* watch your organization go down in flames.

At a recent seminar in Boston, Dr. Covey gave the example of trying to navigate the streets of Boston by using a map of Hartford, Connecticut. You may be an excellent map-reader, but **if either your compass** *or* **your map is flawed... you're in serious trouble.**

In the 1998 Eco-Challenge, a team of four of the world's most talented athletes learned this the hard way. The Eco-Challenge took them 300 miles, kayaking a fierce ocean, running, climbing and mountain biking the Moroccan desert.

The team reached the summit of a 15,000 foot peak, only to look out over the desert and realize they were *one peak off!* Imagine the emotional devastation -- having survived and conquered, only to realize that a valley separated them from their intended destination!

According to Dr. Covey, even dramatic improvements in Total Quality Management (TQM}, or customer service, will *fail* to correct the underlying problem if you lack a common vision. If you don't agree upon your destination, it's certain you'll never get there.

Dr. Dru Lebby warns of a classic formula for corporate doom. Lebby alludes to the lifecycle curve that describes the birth, life and death of any product, organization or for that matter, civilization. Take, for example, VCRs. Initially (point A), only a few were produced, costing tens of thousands of dollars each. Only the major broadcast networks could afford them.

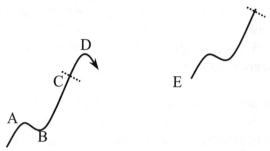

Then, after a short lull (dip in the curve, point B), VCRs caught on. Increased popularity justified mass production that accounted for a drastic reduction in price and subsequent exponential growth of the product. Things are going great, right?

Dr. Lebby attributes the eventual demise of every great organization to the belief that more of the same is better. How many hot computer companies *buried* themselves by sticking to what had always worked in the past? "Abandon everything" sound familiar?

Follow the curve beyond the exponential growth to see the crash (point D and beyond). Why do they all crash? Lebby attributes it to extreme shortsightedness on the part of the corporate planners. We all have a tendency to pour R & D money onto the *wrong* part of the curve.

Lebby argues that we should 'jump curves' in the heat of the fire (point C). Just when things couldn't be more explosive (see the dotted line), we should **move on**. Identify and embrace the 'next curve.'

In Unleashing the Killer App, authors Larry Downes and Chunka Mui speak of companies *cannibalizing* themselves – in order not to be 'bumped off' by another's introduction of a *killer app* (killer application).

So the next 'curve' is your own next 'killer app.' Just what Gates was thinking when he demanded that his entire R&D force wipe out hard drives containing *hundreds* of millions of dollars worth of research.

What happened to VCRs? They're past point C, on the way to point D and beyond. Beyond market saturation. *And* at the mercy of multiple new "killer apps" waiting to devour them, like DVD, broadband Internet, and re-writable CD, to name a few.

What does any of this have to do with customer
service?  If customer service *is* your product, it's time
to rethink your approach.  If you *don't* think customer
service pertains to you, think *again*.  Unless you
function inside a vacuum, you're in it, too.

There's good and bad news about how customer
service will affect your bottom line.  First the bad.
**The buzzwords *used to be* TQM** (the *old* curve).
Total Quality Management *was* enough to launch a
business in the Eighties and catapult it into the mid-
Nineties.  So what happened?  As they approached the
year 2000, **why did so many businesses hit the wall?**

Whether the business is health care or computer sales,
in Tokyo or Framingham, Massachusetts, customers
expect far *more* than just quality: they *assume* you'll
deliver quality.

So what's the good news?  It's a *secret*.  Come close.
In the chapters to come, **we'll explore success secrets
of customer service legends** like *Nordstrom, The Ritz
Carlton, Infiniti,* and others.  You'll see that the good
news is that it really won't take rocket science to get
*your business* head and shoulders above the crowd.
That's because *so* **few businesses** (regardless of
size) **understand and *practice* "extreme" customer
service.**

Many years ago, my dad said that my early success
was *not* due to my particular level of quality care, *or*
customer service.  He said, quite bluntly, that I "looked
good," mainly due to others in my field not "looking"
at all.  My friend, Alan Bernstein, (Publisher of *The
Practice Builder*, Irvine, CA) summed it up, **"In the
land of the blind, the one-eyed man is king!"**

I hope you'll enjoy the anecdotes to follow. *However,* **passive reading will rob you of the potential** *windfall* extreme customer service may deliver. At the end of each chapter, *pause* for a moment. No matter how extreme or foreign the concepts, answer the following questions: "What's the "take-home" lesson for me? What levels of *extreme* can *I* practice along the very same lines?"

**Caution**: Lest you think that the *extremely* poor service anecdotes would *never* apply in *your* excellent organization, skip directly to the chapter entitled, "A Matter of Policy (You *Lose*)." No doubt the Management at this delightful establishment would have had heart failure, had they been present!

Enjoy <u>Extreme</u>, and *please* let me know if *you* have a story to share. If you have an example of *Extreme* customer service (for better, or for worse) please contact me through Gems Publishing, USA. 1-888-880-GEMS, *"Ask the Gems Guy"* at www.1000gems.com, e-mail: <u>tom@1000gems.com</u>, fax: 508-861-1550, or write c/o Gems Publishing, USA, 12 Walnut St., Framingham, MA, 01702, USA. Oh – I'm *not* promising that I won't tell *anyone* else!

Tom Orent, D.M.D.

## There Should *be* no 'First-Class'

It hit me like a ton of bricks. There should *be* no 'first-class!' Sure, I'm writing this from a seat located in a section *labeled* 'first-class.' First-class: the airline's realization that *some* people like to be treated a little extra specially.

Some people? Only some people enjoy VIP five-star, *extreme* customer service? Have you ever met *anyone* who *didn't* enjoy being treated as if they were flying 'first-class?' Me neither.

What's first-class air travel all about, anyway? Six inches of additional legroom, a drink or two, and food you can identify. Oh yes, and a better attendant-to-traveler ratio. Sure, they let you board before everyone else. But that's no bargain! Why would anyone want to be on the plane any *longer* than absolutely necessary?

I'm currently on the first leg of a flight to Kelowna, BC. Tomorrow, I'll present a seven-hour seminar and head back to Boston that night. The *only* reason I'm sitting in this section is a ticketing fluke: my trip logistics required the same fee for first-class as coach seating. So I was bumped up. *Otherwise*, it's my commitment to those who hire me to save them unnecessary expense.

But let's go back to taking a closer look at the biggest benefit of flying in first-class – the service. Mind you, it's not what *I'd* call extreme; it is, however, better than what they give you in the back of the plane. Have you ever tried to get the timing down (in coach) so that there's something to drink with your meal?

The meal cart usually precedes the drink cart by about ten rows (or 30 minutes). You can either let the food age in front of you, *or*, consider your soda an 'after dinner drink.'

In first-class seats, you get your drink at the same time as the meal.

There's also the little matter of check-in lines. There may be a queue of 50 people waiting to check in for coach. Yet there's an agent *just* for you, if your seat number is low enough.

"Another drink?"   *"Anything else?"*   "How 'bout today's edition of the *Journal* (WSJ)?"

So why do people pay an enormous difference for the ride up front?  **It's *mostly* a belief that they'll be *treated* extra specially.**

I've been 'accidentally' treated to a first-class ticket a number of times in my career. I've *yet* to be blown away by an example of anything I'd consider representative of *Extreme* Customer Service.

The reality is simple: *extreme* customer service is even *more* impressive when delivered to those sitting in the back *Everyone* loves to be treated as if they *were* in first-class. All you need do is adopt a "Yes" attitude that *exudes* an eagerness to burst at every seam with the *extreme*.

## I'll Meet You at the Mall

It was time to print another run of special reports. The Nameless Copy Business had always done them for me. Open 24x7: you can't beat the convenience. They always did a nice job...*eventually*. You see, they almost always screwed up *some* part of the process.

Why *didn't* they get the order? Why, when the job was completed, were they unable to *find* it? When they moved to a brand-new location, I was certain they'd overcome their inability to properly catalog completed jobs. Wrong.

"The computer shows that the job *is* complete. It's just that I'm having a little trouble locating it right now."

Recently, I arrived to find that one job had *not* been completed on time, as promised. I explained that I needed the materials for a trade show, and a very tight window of time within which to ship.

"We'll have the driver get that to you first thing tomorrow morning."

Sometimes he'd show, other times he wouldn't. Last week, I asked to have 2,000 copies on a particular colored stock. I even showed the young man a sample of one they'd done previously. The next morning, I arrived to pick up the order, which turned out to be 2,000 copies on the *wrong* colored stock.

The manager asked if I wanted them to redo the job. I didn't have the time. "I'm sorry for the mix-up. I'll take 20-percent off the job." I accepted the offer, though clearly this was an example of *extremely weak* customer service.

---

*Extreme* Autopsy

How would you have handled that one? There's a minimum (you can never do too much) solution to make this mix-up right.

Apologize profusely: if you can do this without blaming the staff person responsible, kudos. You're on the right track.

Insist that the customer take the erroneous color (if they are of any use), at no charge. Twenty-percent off was insulting, at best.Tell them how long it will take for you to replace the order with the correct paper. Then figure out a way to make it work logistically for the customer. In my case, I just didn't have time to wait around, or to come back. But, if the manager had offered to rerun the copies at no charge, and arrange for drop-off at my office that afternoon – or ship directly to the convention site – at her expense... now that would have worked for me.

---

When service, communication, or quality of results breaks down (these people were batting zero for three), opportunity knocks for a competitor somewhere nearby. Enter Robert.

Robert used to work for the Nameless Copy Business and I enjoyed dealing with him. He almost always got the order right the first time; he was very confident, and quite knowledgeable about his business.

One day, when I was picking up some office supplies, I bumped into Robert. His new job was managing Copy Max, the copy and printing department of Office Max.

"Hi, Tom, how've you been?"

"Robert! How are *you*?"

"Great! Tom, I'm running Copy Max, now, and would really appreciate giving us a try some time. You know I'll really take good care of you." I told Robert that, next chance I got, I'd bring something his way.

Combine my routinely mediocre experiences at the Nameless Copy Business with Robert's *attitude* and guess where I brought the next batch of special reports?

Though not rocket science, the job wasn't straightforward copying. The report required a full color cover, generated from a file on disc; thirty pages of straight copying; a black vinyl back; clear cover; and special binding. I needed 100 copies for this particular run.

A job like that wouldn't be inexpensive, so I figured I'd have the Nameless Copy Business give me a quote *before* I handed it over to Robert at Copy Max. At least I'd have some basis for comparison. I'd already anticipated that if Robert could deliver a quality product, on time, I'd prefer to work with him. Price was *not* the primary issue, but it *did* turn out to be a nice, additional benefit.

One Friday afternoon, about two weeks after I rediscovered Robert, I showed up with my order in-hand. He seemed genuinely *delighted* to see me again. Two points for him. You'd display similar feelings for a guest arriving at your home, wouldn't you?

Why not do likewise for *every* person with whom you do business? There really shouldn't be any 'first-class!'

I had the quote from the Nameless Copy Business in my pocket. If it had come close, we'd do business. The Nameless Copy Business wanted $647.00 for the job.

Robert thanked me for coming in, and for the opportunity to quote the job. We reviewed the job together. Nameless Copy Business had produced a single color, laser master, and all the rest were color copies of the original laser output. Robert said he would produce *all* 100 covers from the disc. No color copies. All originals. I liked his style already.

The rest of the job would be done in a manner similar to his competitor. He took his time, carefully reviewing each facet of the job before coming up with his quote. "Tom, the total will be $479.00. I can have these ready for you on Monday."

What a deal! He promised better quality covers, a couple-of-days turnaround, and enormous savings over the competition! The job was his. I left him my cell phone number, in case of unforeseen questions or problems, and bid him a good day.

As I was about to leave, Robert grabbed a store flyer and said, "Wait, just a second. I'm also going to give you one of these coupons for $25.00 off!" Even with the deal already closed, he was taking *another* $25.00 off the price!

Monday morning arrived and I'd not heard from Robert. The job must be all set (or so I'd hoped). On my way out, I grabbed my cell phone: there was a message waiting. "Hi Tom, this is Robert. I'm sorry, but your job is not ready yet. We had a small problem with the binding and I'll need to speak to you as soon as you're able."

I dialed his number on my way out the door. I anticipated yet another example like the old Nameless Copy Business' *extremely* mediocre customer service.

"Tom, I'm so glad you called. Everything is printed, but the machine that does our binding broke down, and it won't be repaired for about two weeks."

I envisioned bringing 3,000 loose sheets over to Nameless Copy Business, crawling on my hands and knees before them. Having to face the manager with the "No, we can't" attitude, and ask *her* for a favor?! I couldn't wait two weeks. A good portion of the order was to be shipped out in two days for a trade shows.

"So what can we do, Robert?"

"Well, I've taken the liberty of making up samples of two other types of binding. I'd like you to take a look at them. Where are you right now?"

"I'm in my car, on the way to lunch."

"*Where* are you going for lunch?"

"The Natick Mall food court."

"Would it be okay if I were to *meet* you there, with the samples?"

*Would* it? *That's* the kind of recovery I love to see. If handled properly, recovery can be *better* than doing it right the *first* time.

We met at the Mall. Robert showed me the two completed bound reports. One looked too cheap for my publication. The other was a beautifully done, cloth binder, similar to old-fashioned bookbinding. It was certainly a cut *above* what I'd been used to. But would he be willing to do 100 at the same price as the originally quoted process?

"Tom, there *is* a difference in price for the cloth binding." Didn't you just *know* that was coming? I felt like a shopper responding to a deal "too good to be true". Bait and switch. Too bad. Up to this point, all had gone well (except the fact that it was Monday and the job wasn't done yet).

Before I had a chance to respond, Robert finished, "The total job will run $75.00 *less* if we use the cloth." I thought I'd misunderstood. The cloth looked far more professional than the plastic binder he'd promised, and would cost $75.00 *less?*

Let's recap what's happened so far:

1) I'm greeted and *treated* as if he *cares* if I come back. At Nameless Copy Business, I'd done close to $10,000.00 business with them, and *never* felt particularly well treated.

2) For $168.00 *less,* he's offered to give me *original* quality covers instead of copies.

3) *After* the sale was made, he produced a coupon for an *additional* $25.00 off.

4) First thing Monday morning, he called to let me know of the glitch. He offered to *meet* me wherever I wanted, to show me two alternatives he'd *already* put together.

5) What appears to be a nicer looking binding will save me *another* $75.00!

I thanked him for his efforts, and he promised to have the job completed by the next morning.

The next night, I went back to Copy Max to pick up the order. No Robert. A young man was behind the counter, alone. I knew the order would be ready, but was concerned that the young man might not price it as Robert had promised.

"Hi, I'm here to pick up some reports that Robert did for me."

"Dr. Orent?"

Ten feet tall. That's how you feel when you're called by name, by someone who's never met you... *before* you have a chance to tell them who you are!

I was truly impressed. The simple use of my name said volumes: I knew that he *expected* me. That put my mind at rest. I knew it meant that Robert had gone over the job ticket with him, and that Robert had *anticipated* the possibility that he might not be there when I came by.

"Yes."

---

*Extreme* Autopsy

We do something similar at the Center for Esthetic Dentistry. A new female patient is scheduled to arrive at 2:40 p.m. An unfamiliar face presents to the reception desk at 2:30 p.m. Before she has a chance to tell us who she is, and why she's here, she is greeted: "Hi, Mrs. Barton, I'm Cecilia. It's a pleasure to have you with us. Welcome."

Is it possible that this is yet *another* unfamiliar face, perhaps a "walk-in" patient? Sure, but the odds are in our favor, and we'll gamble *every* time. It's a far cry from so many physicians' offices where bulletproof glass isolates the staff, and the sign at the front desk reads, "Please enter your name and have a seat."

---

"Great. Robert left me instructions. Your job is all set. It looks wonderful." And indeed it did. It was far nicer than the previous run done by Nameless Copy Business. The original color covers and cloth binding added a touch of class to the report.

"Robert asked me to explain to you that he made an error in estimating the price." Uh oh. Otherwise known as "the other shoe drops." I had a brief moment of weakness in the knees.

"He mentioned a coupon for $25.00 off?"

"Yes..." I hoped that this was the *only* error he'd made. The price seemed far too low for the quality result, and the service I'd received. Perhaps it would get him in trouble if he applied the coupon. Though I wasn't thrilled, I could live without the $25.00 off.

"Robert misread the coupon. It was *not* for $25.00 off. It was for twenty-five *percent* off!"

Too good to be true? Nope. With the tax, I paid just over $300.00 for the job! Where do you think I'll direct my business the next time I need similar services? And you can *bet* I'll refer folks his way in a heartbeat.

*Editor's Note:  Since this story was first written, Robert left Copy Max to start up his own printing company, Digital Express, in Framingham, Massachusetts. He has maintained his extraordinarily high level of enthusiasm for going above and beyond routine customer service.*

## Mary and Ali

On the Delta shuttle, from Boston, I overheard someone say, "New York – with me it's a *love/hate* relationship." That about sums it up for me, as well. When I think of life in New York, I imagine driving a brand new Lexus – in a demolition derby. It's a great car. What a *waste* to take it to *that* horror show.

I was lecturing to the First District Dental Society of New York, the next day. I arrived at the Grand Hyatt, at Park Avenue and Grand Central. I was anxious to drop my bags (two suits, my laptop, and six carousels of lecture slides) and get to my dinner meeting. Check in is a *moment of truth* – "make it or break it" for a hotel. After all, this *is* the first impression (okay, not really *the* first, but one of them).

There were about ten people ahead of me, but the registration desk was fairly long, and there was numerous staff on duty. I was optimistic. Each of the guests ahead of me took quite some time to check in; one represented a group of 15, on tour from Brazil.

It took about 15 minutes before I heard, "Next in line?" After being 'processed' by the airlines, waiting 15 minutes to register is like five minutes on telephone hold. Poor Mary didn't know *what* she was getting. I'm not the easiest person to please when things are average, let alone after this type of wait.

Mary said, "Good evening, sir. I'm so sorry about the wait. How long *were* you waiting?"

"About 20 minutes, I guess." You see, at this point I wanted sympathy, and Mary struck a chord with her greeting. Talk about diffusing a bad situation. I couldn't help but appreciate her seemingly genuine concern. But then I wondered, was she going to *do* anything with that information, or was it superficial?

"Mary, what are you going to *do* with that information?"

"Well, sir, this is my second day on the Registration desk. I'm taking note of everything I can, so that I can present suggestions for improvements." I don't know if Mary is a manager, shifted temporarily to the desk to improve customer service. Or if, as a brand new employee, she simply approached her *job* as would a management professional.

"Dr. Orent, you're on the *business* floor." Well, I'd heard Dr. Bill Blatchford's explanation of the '*business* floor' concept. Hotels were sacrificing a couple of guestrooms to design a 'business lounge.' Guests could work in the lounge, use the fax machine, or just relax there. Only the 'business floor' guests' keys fit the private slots in the elevator – making them feel pretty important.

I asked her for the rate. Initially, my travel agent had quoted a one-night rate of $335.00; I asked her to try harder, and, that day, my rate for the same room dropped to $265.00.

Mary responded, "Your rate, Dr. Orent, is $265.00."

"Is $265.00 your least expensive rate?"

"No," she replied, "we do have a room on another floor, for $250.00."

"And what's the difference between the business floor room, and this room?"

"The business floor includes free local phone calls." I didn't intend to call (nor did I even know) anyone in the city. "*And*, the business floor includes a free continental breakfast."

"I don't eat before I lecture, and won't use the phone. Would you please move me *off* the business floor?"

"Dr. Orent, I'm going to *leave* you on the business floor, but still *give* you the lowest rate – the $240.00."

Not brain surgery, but Mary took a negative start and made it into a pretty nice start. *Not* "extreme," but a "nice start."

A bellman, named Ali, took my bags. "My name is Ali, sir, Ali," and he pointed to his nametag. Smart move: I'd *hear* his name, and then *see* his name. Since he took a separate service elevator, I'd remember him, in the unlikely event we weren't quickly reunited.

There was another very subtle, but nice touch from Ali; as he placed the bags in my room, he said, "You've been with us *before*, sir." Well, I did feel special that they'd made special note, or remembered that I had indeed been there once, a few years back.

But wait! It took a few moments to process this one...

---

*Extreme* Autopsy

Ali had used a line we, too, employ, at the Center for
Esthetic Dentistry!  A patient is on the phone, and our
team member doesn't recognize the name.  If you
don't recognize a name, and *ask*, "Have you been
here before?" you may offend someone who *has*, in
fact, been a very good patient for years.  Instead, we
ask, "Roughly, when was the last time you visited us?"
Ali's version was appropriate for his type of business:
"You've been with us *before*, sir."

---

Either way you phrase it, you win. A current client (or
hotel guest, in this case) will answer the question. A
new client or customer will simply respond that this is
their very first time with you.  As my dear friend, the
Texas rancher and entrepreneur, Walter Hailey, says,
"MMFI – **make me feel important!**"

## The "Organization" Organization

When I think of Franklin-Covey, the word "organization" immediately comes to mind. Dr. Stephen Covey wrote the best-selling 7 Habits of Highly Effective People – the book **directly responsible for my success in publishing.** Before reading Dr. Covey's book, I'd never have dreamed of **finding the time** to author three books, a video tape and cassette series, special reports, numerous articles, and an audio book on cassettes... while maintaining my full-time dental practice!

The other half of the highly successful Franklin-Covey duo comes from Franklin Quest – the Franklin Planner people. During the last decade, C.E.O. Hyrum Smith, and his company, have trained tens of thousands in the art of "life management." Mr. Smith begins his seminar with a very powerful promise: he *guarantees* that, if you follow his principles for 21 days, **his time management seminar will change your life.** It will dramatically improve your productivity in your personal and professional lives, *and* bring you a sense of peace and fulfillment.

Already an *extreme* Covey fan, and impressed by Mr. Smith's lectures, I made the decision to purchase my very own Franklin Planner. If you've never owned (and used) a planner, I should warn you – the **decision to purchase a planner is not unlike deciding to have another child!**

Conception was Saturday, November 29, 1997, 10:02 a.m. The planner was delivered only a few hours later. Conception to delivery is remarkably swift, and relatively painless. I *would* have another. It was a healthy baby Franklin Planner. Pocket-sized!

I couldn't wait to hear the tapes (a wonderful four-cassette seminar comes with the deluxe planner). I ripped open the box, and started to listen on the ride home. The **potentially life-revolutionizing information** in those four tapes (and with the help of the planner, as a tool) is **mind boggling**.

As Mr. Smith promised, he doesn't just teach *time* management. The seminar provides a **laser-like path to the clarification and subsequent fulfillment of lifetime dreams**. How many people have taken the time and expended the effort to document their core values and lifetime goals? Less than a few percent. How many of *those* have a time-tested plan to maintain their values and achieve their goals?

So there I was, Saturday afternoon – a man with a mission. I'd listened to the seminar, and read the accompanying manuals. I laid out *all* the materials, and assembled my new baby (you've figured, by now, the Franklin Planner isn't just another calendar!). I was ready to begin planning. **The materials were everything the *organization* had promised**, and more – or *less*...

I was ready to condense and focus my three calendars, random notepads, and 40 or 50 pieces of what Mr. Smith calls 'floating papers' – but something was missing. I was devastated.

There was no December 1997! **I'd have to wait a *month* to play with my new baby!**

The planner begins with the *next* quarter! How could this be? I'm ready *now!* I ran to my computer and sent off an *urgent* fax to Mr. Smith. I explained how, with sweaty palms, I'd corralled my calendars and floating papers... and was prepared to commence to condense! Thwarted, my December was gone!

I figured that surely Franklin-Covey would come through. They *had* to! They were the *organization* organization! Of all the companies on the planet, *they* would understand.

**Day One after the urgent fax**: I decided to go to work that day. Even without December. After all, when anticipating any event the magnitude of a birth, you need something to keep your mind occupied. I went to work – and alerted my staff to notify me if an urgent return phone call (or fax) was to come in from a Hyrum  Smith. I went to bed that night disappointed, but hopeful.

**Day Two after the fax**: How could this be? Was it possible that Franklin-Covey would let me down? I thought not. In fact, since Day One, I'd formulated a picture in my mind of *exactly* what must be going on...

The fax had arrived at FC (Franklin-Covey). As it finished transmitting, and the automatic paper cutter sheared it free, there must have been a **key employee** *right* there (the one **responsible for the immediate deployment of the UFRT** – "Urgent Fax Response Team").

She grabs the fax, and heads toward the executive offices – reading the fax header as she *runs*. Identifying the urgent fax as an incoming for the CEO, she takes a hard left turn and stops abruptly at Mr. Smith's office. Having scanned the fax, and realizing the urgency, she enters the office, *without* wasting precious moments to knock.

"Mr. Smith, I'm so sorry to interrupt your meeting. But sir, there's an urgent fax from a newcomer. Sir, could you read it, *now?*"

Smith checks his planner, and replies, "You're the new UFRT leader?"

"Yes, sir."

"Nicely done. I've got 33 seconds. Let me see the fax. *Now.*"

The UFRT leader immediately places the fax in front of the CEO. He skims the fax in a matter of 11 seconds, leaving 22 seconds to fire the following command: "December, '97 filler pages... FedEx, *next* day delivery... *GO!*"

**10:25 a.m., Day Two**: The FedEx arrived! I'd like to believe that it happened just as I imagined. Of course I have no clue *how* they did it. To borrow one of Tom Peters' favorite words, I've had **a *'wow'* experience with Franklin-Covey**.

"SHE GRABS THE FAX, AND HEADS TOWARD THE EXECUTIVE OFFICES.-- READING THE FAX HEADER AS SHE RUNS..."

## About Your Phone

Before NASA sends an astronaut out for a jaunt around the shuttle, how much time and effort do you think they put into *their* lifelines?

That 'umbilical' cord, which tethers the astronaut to the ship, represents the difference between *life and death* for the folks in spacesuits. Millions of dollars and untold years of research and development precede any live use of those lines.

What about *your* lifelines? Does a computer answer *your* phones? Sure, it's cheaper. The computer answers multiple lines simultaneously. Answers on the first ring! That's great! But what about the *human* being at the calling end of the line?

Did you ever stop to think about your *customers'* feelings about your 'automated operators?'

Trying to navigate some of these systems is similar to finding your way around the paved cow-paths in downtown Boston! According to legend, city 'planners' in Boston simply laid asphalt wherever the cows had roamed! I swear there's a place in downtown Boston where four one-way streets intersect – *all* meet (and *end*) in the intersection! There's no way out!

Isn't that how it feels after you've tried, unsuccessfully to navigate some company's electronic phone maiden? "Thank you for calling 'XYZ' corporation. Please listen carefully, and choose from the following menu: If you know your party's extension, you may dial it at any time. Simply enter the following sequence, first: '4-3-5-1-7-2-6', followed by their nine-digit extension. If, perchance, you reach the correct party, hit the 'pound' key twice followed by '0-0'. If you do not know your party's extension, please choose from the following fifty-one selections..." Just once, I'd like to meet, face to face, with the design engineer... Yes, it's cheaper. But is it, *really*?

Yes, it will *cost* more to have operators answer your phones. So a customer satisfaction survey might not be a bad idea. Perhaps it would be worthwhile to hire a focus group. Do you have any idea how many people hang up? Get frustrated? Develop an *attitude?* Here's a thought. Ask the folks who program your system to add one more option: prior to forwarding the call, have the system ask the following: "If you'd like to comment on our use of the automatic operator, instead of a human being, press..."

Though "Hold, please" isn't *extreme*, it *is* extremely rude. If you'd like your party to hold, *ASK IF HE/SHE MINDS HOLDING!* It takes so very little effort to say and do the right thing. And one more pet peeve: if you ask if the caller can hold, *WAIT for an ANSWER!* Every so often I'm greeted with, "ABC Corporation, would you mind holding?" Click. Click. The first click was the incredibly rude operator putting me on hold, *prior* to waiting for my reply. The second click was (you guessed it) me hanging up!

And what about when you *do* place callers on hold? What do they listen to? If you say "Nothing," you lose. Allowing your valuable customers to wait on hold, listening to silence, is dangerous.

What's wrong with silence? Everything. First, it's boring. If you have me listening to something, *anything*, I'm less likely to concentrate on how long you've ignored me than if I'm listening to my own heartbeat through the phone's earpiece.

Your options for on-hold silence breakers include "information-on-hold" services, or music. Music, if played off of a radio patch, can be very dangerous, as well. Why? Put yourself in *the caller's* shoes. You've called XYZ company (your company) to find out what time they close this evening. You've been placed on hold…a *long* hold.

Just when you (as the caller) are about to give up on XYZ, the radio announcer mentions that ABC Company (your competitor!) always provides *terrific* service, and is open tonight until ten! Well, you gave your caller "information on hold," just not exactly the *type* of information you'd like to offer.

There's another reason *not* to use any form of music on-hold. Your customer may *hate* your selection. Yes, *hate*. Country music fans (of which there are *many*, though one would never know it up here in the Northeast) are *crazy* in-love with their music.

Others don't care for Country (this was put mildly in order to keep the PG rating on this book). Why take the chance of really turning off your customers with music they can't stand. Consider "information-on-hold" systems. Your customers *know* they're on-hold. *You* have complete control over the content.   You *don't* want to hard sell.  Rather, the ideal on-hold information would be useful, free information or valuable advice.

Some of the most successful companies on the Internet became successful by *giving* something of value, for free.  Bill Gates *gave* Windows to IBM, in order to strengthen Microsoft's position in the industry.  IBM, Microsoft, *and* the end-user won.  All got something of value that they could use.

At a recent dental seminar, I asked the audience what percentage of the American population has some level of chronic gum infection.  The answer?  More than 80 percent.   I followed with, "What percentage of the American population do you think: a) knows the prevalence of the problem; and b), understands the steps necessary to combat it – in order that they might prevent unnecessary tooth-loss?"

Only a tiny fraction of adult Americans are aware they have a problem, or understand the correlation between chronic gum infection, bone loss, and the loss of their teeth.  That would certainly be one possible use of an "information on-hold" system.

What if you owned a retail tire outlet?   What percentage of folks do you think remember to check the air in their tires on a routine basis?  If they realized how much money it might save them (allowing for proper tire wear), they might check them *today*.  You might even consider finding statistics, from the National Transportation Safety Administration, concerning the annual number of fatalities linked to tires with excessive wear.

Information-on-hold can benefit *everyone*. Give away as much information as possible. In addition to the immeasurable goodwill you'll create, you'll likely see a direct increase in sales as a result, as well.

One award-winning Ohio-based Company providing such a service is Sold-On-Hold-Productions. For information, contact Mr. Ron Smith, at 614-525-3535 (or fax, 614-899-2329). Due to recent advances in digital technology, you can be up and running, from scripting, to production *and* equipment, with total packages starting *well* under $1,000.00.

## Lexus!

In 1992, when Dr. Lee Ofner visited Kuni Lexus in Denver, Colorado, he had no idea he was in for a dose of *extreme* **customer service** – *Lexus* **style!** Sales consultant Pam Farris offered just the right level of attention – answering questions, when asked, yet allowing time alone to appreciate Lexus' quality.

When all was said and done, Dr. Ofner drove home in a brand-new 1992 LS 400. His distinctive new Lexus was everything he'd hoped for, and more. It was flawless. Initially.

**11,000 miles later:** Dr. Ofner and his son drove 60 miles, from their home, in Colorado Springs, to Denver to attend a high school basketball tournament. While in Denver, they decided to visit Kuni Lexus, to check the front right tire that seemed substantially more worn than the others.

The Ofners arrived in Denver an hour before the tournament was to begin. The Kuni service supervisor took them right in, cautioning it might take more than a quick look to determine the *cause* of the problem. He asked if they had time to wait. No, the tournament was due to start and they didn't want to miss a second.

The **supervisor gave them the keys to a Lexus LS 300, and told them to enjoy the tournament!** It snowed Colorado-style that night; they stayed overnight in Denver.

The next morning, Lexus still wasn't satisfied, and told the Ofners they'd like to keep the car a bit longer.  Dr. Ofner and his son returned home to Colorado Springs, in the LS 300: the dealer told them to keep it as long as needed!

**The next day their LS 400 was *delivered* (120 miles roundtrip) to their home!**  Although Dr. Ofner's concern was with one tire, **the dealership took the liberty of giving him four brand new tires.  *No charge!***

But this example of *extreme* customer service didn't end there.  Lexus apparently did *not* solve the underlying problem – the *cause* of the unusual tire wear.

**12,000 additional miles later** (23,000 miles *old*), the Ofners returned to the dealer once again – **and again received four more brand new tires, at *no charge!***

This time, Lexus solved the mal-alignment responsible.  The second *free* set of tires lasted several years, the remaining time Dr. Ofner owned the vehicle.

## Pass it ON. *Please!*

More about the phone. John calls in with a complaint. He's been a great customer for ten years. This is the first time he's had occasion to share a minor (at this point) grievance.

"Strickland Widgets. This is Mary speaking, how may I direct your call?"

"Hi, my name is John White. I'm in charge of procurement for Berriman Steel Corporation. We just received a shipment of two million widgets, which, unfortunately, are the wrong part numbers. We were looking for the '1-2-3,' and you shipped '3-2-1' to us."

"Mr. White, could you please hold?"

"Certainly."

A few moments later. "Hi this is Bill, in shipping and receiving, may I help you?"

"Well, er, yes. Did Mary explain my problem?"

"Mary?"

"Mary. The *operator.*"

"Oh, yes, of course. *Mary.* Nope."

"Look, my name is John White.  I'm in charge of procurement for Berriman Steel Corporation.  We just received a shipment of two million widgets, which, unfortunately, are the wrong part numbers.  We were looking for the '1-2-3', and you shipped '3-2-1' to us."

"Oh, you're with Berriman.  I remember that order. Just a minute.  I'm going to transfer you to Richard Smith, our product supervisor.  Could you hold for just a moment?"

---

*Extreme* Autopsy
You might imagine (correctly), that when Mr. Smith picks up, he's going to be *clueless,* as well.  And Mr. White, should at that point, be "loaded for bear"!

---

*If* you have been given information (even if it's more information than you wanted to know) ***pass it on!*** The above encounter is *not* an exaggeration. If anything, it's *understated*.  It *is extreme*. Extremely rude. On numerous occasions, I've told the same sad story to three or four people, up the chain of command!

Done correctly, it should have sounded something like this: "Hi, Mr. White. This is Bill, in Shipping. I'm sorry to hear there was an error in shipping your '1-2-3' widgets. May I transfer you to Richard Smith, our product supervisor? I'm certain Mr. Smith can help straighten this out, pronto. By the way, I'm the one who actually loads the product, so I'll keep my eye on the new order, and give it kid glove attention. Sorry, again, about your trouble. Could you please hold for Mr. Smith?"

You'd better believe that when Richard Smith picks up, he'll start off with a greeting (using Mr. White's name), an apology, *and* how and *when* the matter will be resolved.

*Please, pass it on!*

## Personal Touch

Extreme excellent customer service is rarer, yet even *more* important, for the 'big guys.' Here, the personal touch goes a very long way.

The folks at Radio Shack are very savvy about the latest, greatest tools and toys. Their slogan, "You've got questions, we've got answers" is personified by Mike, at their Natick, Massachusetts location. Mike got me up and running on Sprint PCS. He'd even call me if there were better deals on something I'd recently purchased (then he'd *do* something about it). He made me feel as if I had a seven figure stock portfolio with his company (not just a $125.00 phone)!

I was lecturing in Hawaii. Mike had switched me over to Sprint PCS, recently, upgrading to digital technology. At that time, Sprint was up-front about the state of their network: the system had holes here and there, but was offering a great entry-level deal for customers willing to bear with occasional glitches.

In Honolulu, I tried to use my new digital phone. Sprint PCS was not available there yet, and roaming wouldn't work. I called the local Hawaiian cellular company; they, in turn, contacted Sprint PCS to check on the roaming contracts and technological capabilities of their phones. It was determined that this was something Sprint PCS would have to do from their end.

I knew I wouldn't be using my phone for the duration, and doubted I'd hear about it again. To my surprise (and *extreme* delight), there was a message on my home voice-mail.

"Hi Dr. Orent, this is Chris, at Sprint PCS technical support. I'm very sorry for the inconvenience while you were in Hawaii. We appreciate your getting the ball rolling with your phone call.

"In two weeks, please look for the "version 216 upgrade; it will be available, at no charge, to Sprint PCS users. The upgrade will allow users to roam in Hawaii and many other locations. Once again, sorry for the inconvenience. If you have any further questions or problems, please call me personally. You can reach me toll-free, at, 800..."

---

*Extreme* Autopsy

Is *your* follow-up *that* sharp?   Multinational or mom and pop, you can't afford *not* to look that great.

## Foresight = *WOW*

Marketing guru Dan Kennedy has logged more air miles than NASA's shuttle commanders. Dan is a prolific writer. He teaches others how to capture the attention of their target markets – and what to do once they're listening.

In this chapter, Dan describes the *Extreme* customer service he received on one of his seminar trips. Long frequent travels can be exhausting. *This* type of service turns travel into an enjoyable journey...

You know I travel a great deal. Most hotels and motels are, frankly, lousy and price doesn't seem to matter.

When I was traveling, doing seminars every night, we worked from 7-10 p.m. Many hotels close their restaurants at 10 o'clock, as did this one, the Marriott Courtyard.

First of all, check-in went smoothly. It was perfect. Second, a staff person was waiting for me at 6 p.m. at the meeting room to be sure everything was the way I wanted it.

Third, at 10:30 p.m., after the seminar, I dragged my tired rear end up front and said, "I know your restaurant's closed, where's the closest place I could get a sandwich and a drink?"

Here's what the guy said. "Well, there are several good places, but because we saw you weren't finishing until 10, we went ahead and made up a couple of ham, turkey and cheese sandwiches, and we saved you a good salad, and we'd be happy to serve you that in the bar, if you like." What a shock! *That* was a WOW experience.

How you replicate that kind of experience, I can't dictate. But, I can tell you that any client who has that kind of experience will automatically refer at a higher level than she or he otherwise would have.

Dan Kennedy is the author of numerous books and a top guru on marketing, advertising, and promotions.   For information of his books, seminars, talks and products, contact him at Inner Circle, 5818 N. Seventh St., Phoenix, AZ 85014. Telephone 800-223-7180.

## A Standard Let-Down

It was one of my longer road trips: a four-city lecture tour, starting in Calgary, and ending up with two dates in Ohio.  Each seminar was seven hours, so I was ready for all the extreme (*positive*) customer service I could get!

Two flights and countless hours after clearing Customs, I arrived at Columbus Airport, in Ohio.  I'd started out in Calgary at 8:00 a.m., and it was 6:00 p.m. when I arrived at the Nameless Car Rental desk.

I was tired and still had a 90-minute drive before I could settle in and prepare for the next lecture.  "Hi, Steve, how are you tonight?"

"Fine, sir, and you?"

"Great, thanks.  A little bit road-worn, but great, thanks."

"How may we help you this evening?"

"I have a car reserved – Orent."

"Yes, Sir.  I've got your ticket right here."

"Great.  Steve, I was wondering if you could possibly give me a courtesy upgrade?"

"Already did, sir."

Now *that's* the way it *should* be handled. When you can anticipate a customer's request, before it leaves their lips, *and* meet or *exceed* their expectations, you're delivering *extreme* customer service. Or so I thought.

"That's terrific. After an all-day travel, I can't tell you how much I appreciate that."

"Had no choice, sir. That's all we had left this evening."

NO question: Steve is an idiot. Try this analogy: you're the home team. Two outs and bases are loaded. You're behind by three runs. Bang! You slam one into the center field bleachers. But wait… while running the bases, you jog over to the wall near first base to give high fives to a couple of excited fans. The umpire calls you *out* for leaving the base path! Now the goat, you *could* have been the hero. All you needed to do was finish what you started.

---

*Extreme* Autopsy

Steve's experience (and thus 'Nameless') was a let down in service that night. It would have been so very simple for him to make me feel special. How might he have handled the same situation, and come out a winner?

"Dr. Orent, it was certainly my pleasure, sir. It's apparent that you have traveled long and hard to get here this evening, and in your shoes, *I* would appreciate an extra VIP touch, as well."

So it's a bit of a stretch. But it still sounds better than, "Had no choice, sir."

## Small Phone, *Extreme* Service

Gabe Bodnar is a typical 'soccer dad.' He loves to get into the action, down on the field, with his son. One bright, Florida morning, he dropped his Motorola Star-Tac phone on the field.

The phone was damaged, out of commission. Gabe took the phone back to the dealer. After examining the phone, the dealer asked him to leave it because they'd have to send it back to Motorola for service.

When asked how long it would be, the dealer promised that Dr. Bodnar would receive a call within seven days, advising him of the phone's status – time needed to repair, costs involved, etc.

*Exactly* seven days later, a rather large FedEx package arrived. Gabe opened the box to find an endless cushion of bubble wrap. Suspended in the center of the wrap was his phone. Repaired, like new.

The enclosed note detailed the repair. Although the damage was obviously not due to a factory defect (unless factory protocol includes stepping on the phone with cleats!) there was no charge. Not *only* was it a courtesy repair, there was no charge for the overnight shipping, either. Zero.

*Extreme* Autopsy

**Customer perception is better than 90% of buying motive,** *as well as* reasons for loyalty after-the-fact.

"OOPS!"

## Shuttle Diplomacy

I arrived at the airport, in Houston, at 11:00 p.m. My contact at Kreativ Corporation (the seminar sponsor) had prepared all travel arrangements, including a neatly detailed itinerary.

I was to catch the shuttle to the Galleria Crown Plaza. The notes indicated a $17.00 one-way fee for the shuttle. I've been taken for enough rides (literally), so it's comforting to know, ahead of time, what to expect to pay.

I picked up my luggage, and it was 11:15 p.m. when I arrived at the City Ground Transportation Desk. I asked where I could pick up the shuttle to the Galleria Crown Plaza.

"Shuttle stops at 11:00 p.m. You'll *have* to take a cab," he said with authority.

"How much for the cab?"

"$42.00."

With the tip, I was looking at a $50.00 bill, one-way! The shuttle pulled up while we were speaking.

"What's that?" I asked.

He actually put his hands up in the air, and told me he didn't know!

I walked over to the 'mystery van.' The lettering on the side rang a clear bell: "Shuttle." I asked the driver if his rounds included the Galleria Crown Plaza. Indeed, they did. He directed me back inside, to purchase a $17.00 ticket at the *Shuttle* Desk!

I met a lovely lady at the Shuttle Desk. I asked what time the shuttle runs 'til. She told me that the last one leaves the airport at 11:30 p.m.

"And furthermore, the city transport folks *know* that!" she said.

When I told her that the City Desk didn't even tell me that there *was* a Shuttle Desk, she wasn't surprised. There are some terrific people working in municipal jobs. It's a shame an uncaring one like that wears the uniform.

---

*Extreme* Autopsy

It wouldn't have taken much to make this a positive (no extreme required) experience. If the City Desk worker knew that the shuttle was still running, then just say so. But give him the benefit of the doubt: assume he really *didn't* know the shuttle schedule.

---

But the possibility that he didn't know about the Shuttle Desk, just inside the doorway, was slim. Have a heart. Share the information and suggest the patron step inside to find out about the shuttle. No extremes needed here, just common decency.

## The Answer is *Yes!*

Want to envelop the epitome of *extreme* customer service? Take your staff to Nordstrom! Unfortunately, the closest Nordstrom to my office is over four hours' drive, in Paramus, New Jersey.

At 6:00 a.m., we loaded into the car, and my dental team and I headed out for a road trip. To Paramus! It sounded like a great idea for a field trip – besides they *love* to shop!

We arrived at Nordstrom just after 10:00 a.m. Ready to shop. Here were the rules: team members received a 50-dollar bill, to spend on themselves. The only requirements were as follows:

1) The 50 dollars must be used for something fun, not practical.

2) They *must* spend it on *themselves.*

3) After each encounter with a Nordstrom employee, *write* down what occurred. What makes them so special?

4) Plan to regroup at noon for lunch in the atrium, and we'll share our 'Nordstrom stories!'

I can't recommend this exercise highly enough! If it's within practicality, take (send) some of your staff on a similar trip. Although the cost and logistics multiply with the increased size of your workforce, so, too, does the dramatic result!   Remember, "In the land of the blind, the one-eyed man is king!"

One of my staff members, Izabel, purchased a pair of socks.   A totally ordinary, inexpensive purchase of socks.   The saleswoman neatly wrapped and bagged the socks (as if they were priceless).   Then a remarkable thing happened when Izabel reached for the bag.

The saleswoman was situated behind a very long counter.   Rather than handing the socks across, she picked up the bag, and walked the length of the counter.   She came around the corner, and back down to where Izabel was standing.   She thanked Izabel for shopping with her, and handed her the bag!

Compare that to experiences we've all had in large department stores, where trying to establish *eye* contact can be a feat in and of itself!

Another team member, Wendy, ventured into the shoe department. The sales force knows just how much room to give; they're always within reach, but *never* imposing.  Wendy was considering a purchase of some moderately expensive shoes.

"Could you tell me what your policy is, for returns?"

"Yes."  Replied the saleswoman.

"Yes?"  Asked Wendy.

"Yes."

At my office, the Center for Esthetic Dentistry, we adopted a policy we affectionately called **"The answer**

**is yes, what's the question?"** We even adorned the lapels of our entire team with brass "YES" pins, to remind us that the answer is *yes*, regardless of the question.

Fact or fiction? One of the oldest Nordstrom stories tells of an elderly woman who returned four worn snow tires. As the legend goes, her dissatisfaction with the tires was enough to warrant Nordstrom's full refund of her money.

Some find it odd that they'd extend such a courtesy, given the time that had obviously elapsed since the purchase. **Most are tickled to learn that Nordstrom has never sold tires of any sort!**

I've asked Nordstrom management if I could peek at their customer service-training manual. They swear it's only one line: "Do *whatever* it takes to *delight* the customer."

---

*Extreme* Autopsy

Regardless of how absurd or bizarre a customer's request, **see if there's some way that you can meet or beat their expectations**. Put yourself in *their* shoes. They wouldn't have *asked* if they didn't have some hope you could oblige.

---

## A Matter of Policy (*You Lose*)

It was a scorching summer day in Newton, Massachusetts. I was a participant in the Massachusetts Baystate Games' Men's Volleyball competition, hosted by a local college.

Nameless Ice Cream has long been a favorite retreat from the heat. They run a little satellite store, inside the University Center, at the local college. Between matches, I ran over to the University Center to bulk up on sorbet.

The day before, I'd had the lemon sorbet with giant carob chips. It was delightful, so I asked for a repeat performance.

"Hi, may I please have a large lemon sorbet, with the giant carob chips?"

"Sorry, we don't have carob chips."

"I got them here, yesterday."

"We don't *have* carob chips."

"I was here yesterday, asked for chocolate chips, and was told *all* you have is carob! A very nice young lady went around back and produced a five-gallon tub filled with chips."

"Oh, **they must have given you the ones we use to bake. We can't** *do* **that.**"

"Please, they were *awesome*. I'd really appreciate some chips."

There were two girls (college age, at best) behind the counter. The one, who'd not yet spoken said to the other, "It's up to you. We don't normally do this. *You can decide if you want to give them to him or not.*"

Have you ever been made to feel like an idiot for no particular reason? The carob chips just became the prize responsible for WWIII!

She pondered her options, took a look at the gathering crowd, and said to me, "Sorry, I'm not able to do that for you. I'm *happy* that you got them yesterday, and that you enjoyed them. But they made an error. We're not supposed to sell the chips used for baking cookies. If you really want them, I'd have to charge you *extra*."

Now we're talking'! "Great! How much for the sorbet with chips?"

"Well, the sorbet is $3.00. I'd have to charge you double. That'd be $6.00."

I was going to have the chips at any cost, until 'any cost' included being made out to be an idiot *and* a fool. Before I could even respond, she added, "If you don't like that, you can go down to our main store in Newton, and speak to the manager."

"What's his name?"

"Stu."

I stepped away from the counter, not defeated, only stunned.  **I was truly in shock at the extent to which these two would go to ruin my sorbet!**

I dialed Information on the cell phone in my pocket, and, moments later, was connected with the main store. Stu was out, but the assistant manager, Gene, stepped in.  He made the immediate (and brilliant) decision that, yes, chips would be fine.  I like it when the executive authority speaks – *especially* in my favor.

Gene asked me to hand the cell phone to Linda, the young lady behind the counter.  When I tried, she told me that I'd have to wait.  She'd already commenced serving the next customer, and would not take the call until through!

She finally took the call.  He implored her to give me chips, and charge a reasonable ($0.75) for them.  In Gene' shoes, I'd have suggested she:

1)  Apologize;
2)  Smother it with chips; and
3)  Give it to me on the house.

No matter.  He may have said just that.  **But Linda wasn't through trying to ruin my sorbet**.  She scooped the sorbet, then headed around the back for the chips.  She placed *exactly* (I counted) eight chips on the sorbet!

When she handed it to me, she said, "I hope this was worth waiting ten minutes for!" Dumb-struck, I stood in amazement, as **she added, "Never again!"**

~ "NEVER AGAIN!"

How simple it would have been to have, then and there, made a new store policy (simple, if management doesn't fire folks for helping customers in this manner). "From today forth, you may have any chips on the premises, for the usual topping fee of $0.75."

The cost of *extremely* poor customer service is *never* just one customer. It is, of course, the ill feelings weathered by all in the store during that episode, along with the many in the volleyball gym within earshot, afterward – and *you!*

---

*Extreme* Autopsy

Either this is a case of two unfeeling and immature young ladies, *or* absentee management abrogating customer service training responsibilities, or *both*. There are some circumstances in which the decision to act in the customer's favor is incredibly obvious: no drawbacks, only positive goodwill to be spread. And yet they screw up. I stand in awe at the lack of caring for another human being, which must exist in the heads of those who'd treat *anyone* this way.

The extreme autopsy, in this case, *cannot* make any suggestions for these two young girls. Well, perhaps, grow up. In a way, it's not really their fault. I *can*, however suggest that if *you* are in a management capacity and thinking of leaving the "store" to the likes of these folks, think *long* and *hard*. We'd be better off to close for a day and do no business, than to subject our reputation to the damage these two must routinely inflict.

---

## The *Extreme* ISP

When I first entered "cyberspace" (the Internet) in 1996, Nameless-On-Line was my ISP (Internet Service Provider). After all, they sent me a free disc in the mail. What could have been any easier?

I soon learned how difficult it was to go beyond the basics with Nameless-On-Line. Yes, it was quick and easy to open an account and get online. However, there's *much* to be desired when it comes to the logic of their address book, and the speed with which mail travels in and out of the system.

I was eventually introduced to my current ISP, Randy Harris. His service, Framingham On-Line (office@framingham.com), is *extreme*. Though he repeatedly surprises me with his personal touch, one night stands out in particular.

I had just emailed him that I was overwhelmed by repeat messages coming off of the server, and didn't have the time to keep downloading them. Randy noticed that I was online at 1:00 a.m.

He read my frustrated cry for help, and mailed me back an invitation to *call* him – at one-o'clock in the morning!

I did, and solved the problem on the spot!

*Extreme* Autopsy

Extreme doesn't know hours.  In fact, any opportunity to reach for the extreme should be seized *as* it presents!

## The Spa

Susan savored the last sips of wine, then laid her head back against the heated pillow as the electronic masseuse soothed sore back muscles of the day gone by. The smell of baking raisin bread filled the air. Stereo headphones piped the opening theme for "My Best Friend's Wedding" – the movie (her request) was just about to begin on the ceiling overhead. She motioned to Izabel to add heat to her lower back. Was she at a Five-Star resort? Perhaps.

During her last stay, she'd been treated to *Guarana*, an imported Brazilian fruit soft drink. That time, the moist heat from the neck pillow really hit the spot: she'd come from a grueling board meeting, downtown. Thus her choice of "Waiting to Exhale," as she sank into the full-length massage pad.

At the end of the visit, to freshen up, Susan is handed a steaming hot, fresh, lemon-scented facecloth. A beautiful basket, overflowing with a wide array of lip-balms, is brought in. Susan chooses the flavor of the day, and treats her lips to a *gourmet* re-moisturization!

A Spa? Of sorts. Susan was indulging in a "Smile Makeover" at the Center for Esthetic Dentistry! *Extreme* customer service rules.

Each of our patients was an invited guest. Our protocol for welcoming a new patient into our practice was similar to welcoming a guest into one's home. We call it our *guest mentality*. It applies, of course to *all* patients, new or return.

**We fashioned our bathroom after the Ritz Carlton, and perhaps offer a few extras *they* don't!** We loved – and adopted – their idea for drying hands after washing. There's nothing quite as luxurious as terrycloth hand towels. A beautiful hutch is lined with freshly laundered towels for each of our special guests.

Atop the hutch is a display of colorful soap oil beads, for patients to admire *or* sample. A basket of potpourri renders a gentle scent in the air. An adjacent lemon candle adds a distant twist to the fragrance. Below are the usual facial tissues and hand creams.

For our patients who were rushed and unable to brush, there's a cup filled with new toothbrushes and sample-sized pastes. From The Body Shop comes a rack of five distinctive body scent atomizers – one of our guests' favorite amenities. For those with leather shoes, an automatic polisher awaits their command.

Many other amenities adorn our guest bathroom. Not a single day goes by without positive comment about our *extreme* facilities!

---

*Extreme* Autopsy

*Extreme* customer service requires thinking in advance, in ways foreign to others in your field. **Less than one-half of one-percent of dentists (polled in my seminars) have set aside feminine products, within reach, in their guest bathrooms.** Ours are in a cabinet discreetly marked with "♀."

---

Oh yes, our guarantee was a bit *extreme,* as well. Most dental offices have *no* written warranty: those that do usually limit coverage for three to five years. Our warranty covered any inlay, onlay, porcelain veneer or crown, as long as I was in practice! We only asked that the patient keep scheduled cleaning and check-up visits, and show up for their appointments.

## May I *Please* Use Your Phone?

Robert Cialdini, Ph.D., in his tape entitled, "Mind Capture," relates one of the most extreme cases of customer service yet. It truly exemplifies the mystical powers your company's "policies" may have over *clueless* employees.

Dr. Cialdini enjoyed working out at his local club. One afternoon, after his workout, he threw his gym bag into the trunk of his car. He dropped his wallet *and* his keys into his gym bag, and proceeded to close the trunk. He didn't even have a quarter for a phone call. Locked out of his car, he said to himself, "Oh, Cialdini, *now* you've done it. Now you're going to have to mildly embarrass yourself by going inside, and saying you locked yourself out of your car."

He went back inside the club. Behind the desk sat the assistant manager, who'd seen him come and go many times over the years. They didn't know each other well, but certainly they'd *acknowledged* each other often.

Cialdini said to the assistant manager, "I feel a little sheepish about this, but I just locked my keys in my trunk. I'm going to need to use one of your phones because I don't have a quarter. I need to call someone to come by with my other set of keys."

The assistant manager looked at Cialdini, and said, "No."

Cialdini, thinking maybe he didn't make himself clear, again explained, "I'm a member here. I've been a member for three years. I don't have a quarter to use your payphone. I don't think you understand. I *need* to use one of your phones."

He said, "**I'm afraid *you* don't understand.** Those phones aren't for the use of our members; they're only for our sales staff to use. And, in fact, a couple of weeks ago, I let one of our members *use* the phone. He abused the privilege; he was on for 45 minutes. My sales manager told me that if I ever let that happen again, it's my hide. **So I'm afraid I can't help you. Sorry." He then turned away**, and started rearranging the towels.

Cialdini was in a *rage*. He said, to himself, "*What?* I'm in need and you've got *three* phones over there. I've been a member for *three* years! That's *it!* Forget it. You've *lost* a customer." He slid his membership card across the desk, turned on his heels, and with great bravado, stomped out of the club.

Of course, he then found himself out in the parking lot, no keys, and no quarter to make the call. First he's locked out of his car. Then, he's *out* of the club he's enjoyed. *They've* lost a customer. He was initially worried about mildly embarrassing *himself; **now** he has to *mortify* himself by *panhandling* for money!*

*Extreme* Autopsy

Cialdini mused about the **simple solutions the assistant manager** *could* **have used** to help him out, and save a customer.

1) The assistant manager could have made the call *for* him!

2) He could have *given* Cialdini a quarter!

3) He could have *loaned* him a quarter. Cialdini would have made the call, been rescued by his friend, and then *repaid* the debt! The assistant manager wouldn't have been out a *penny!*

Robert Cialdini, Ph.D. wrote, <u>Influence, the Psychology of Persuasion</u> (published by Quill). An absolute *must read* book for *anyone* interacting with other humans!

## Sports Talk Radio

Suzanne Boswell has carved a unique niche in the world of customer service analysts: she has come to be known, affectionately, as "The Mystery Patient." Dentists throughout North America recognize her name and logo (her face with a black masquerade mask covering her eyes). The Mystery Patient is equated with customer service excellence.

Ms. Boswell is an author, a lecturer and a consultant. One of her roles is to visit dental practices *incognito*. Dentists who hire her are looking for a true patient's-eye view of their dental organization.

Through focus groups, Ms. Boswell has her finger on the dental consumer pulse. She is able to glean *vital* information to aid those for whom she consults, as well as for her book and seminar audiences.

In her information-*packed* book, The Mystery Patient's Guide to Gaining & Retaining Patients (PennWell Publishing Company), Ms. Boswell relates the following *classic* example of *extreme*ly poor customer service. The following is taken from her chapter, entitled, "Music to Sooth the Savage Beast:"

A woman in one focus group related an incident that I found most unusual. She stated that every time she went to her general dentist, he had a sports talk-radio station playing totally sports all day. The doctor was a sports fanatic and treated a number of local, high profile sports personalities. Though this doctor was known for his clinical skills, the patient became irritated in the office because she was not a sports fan and found the incessant radio chattering to be grating on her nerves.

To make matters worse, the dentist actively was listening to the radio discussions and would periodically voice his own commentary aloud in response to what was being said. The patient found this highly idiosyncratic and, ultimately, it became so irritating that she asked if he would at least change to a music station during her appointment. It was his response that surprised me even more than the unusual situation itself. He said, "Well, I really can't do that. Knowing what's going on in sports is part of my business. I have to be aware of these things for my patients who are involved in sports professionally."

This patient said she left the office and never went back again. Her interpretation was that if the dentist didn't care about her as a person, then her best interests clinically were not taken to heart, either. Her husband had been a patient of the practice, as well. He enjoyed the entire environment, but he also left the practice in support of his wife's viewpoint. It was clear that what was important to the dentist were his *other* patients and his own enjoyment.

---

*Extreme* Autopsy

There are several significant issues to be evaluated here. Is the office tightly focused on the specific demographics of sports enthusiasts or participants? If it is so and particularly if the patient was a non-sports oriented, difficult person, then releasing the patient might be an appropriate recourse for the practice. However, if the practice actively courted a mainstream patient base, then the practitioner might need to take a closer look at his priorities. If these were reasonable patients who were an asset to the practice, whose needs was he meeting – his or his patients? There are times when it is best for the team, and the practice, to have a patient leave. There are also times when it is wise for the practice to accommodate the interests of the patient. This is a subjective issue and must be managed case by case.

---

Bizarre? Perhaps. Sometimes we're so closely focused on our own needs; we fail to entertain the possibility that *others'* aren't served.

Focus groups, mystery patients, and market surveys are but a few of the tools available to *empower* the silent majority to speak. You've often heard that a single complaint represents twenty or more unhappy people. *Seize* the opportunity to *seek out* the complainers and *hear* what they have to offer. It's *not* uncommon for your least enthusiastic customer to become your most ardent supporter, when given proper forum and compassion.

## We Listen. But do we *Really* Hear?

Many years ago, in my practice, we treated a young man named Bob, who was surely the cause of more than one dentist's ulcerated stomach lining. Bob was a young executive with a brokerage firm in downtown Boston. He was **upwardly mobile and outwardly nasty.**

Regardless of how nicely we treated him, at each appointment, he'd *turn* on us -- without fail. Mid-visit, he'd *halt* the treatment, ripping everything out of his mouth. Bob would vault himself up out of the chair, and bury his face in his hands.

He was **verbally abusive to my team and me.** I drew the line, and decided to ask him to leave the practice. The day I confronted him was the *first* day that I began to understand the human side of Bob.

He begged for another chance. Bob told me that this was the first time since childhood he'd ever been able to return to a dentist for treatment. He had painful memories of his childhood dental visits – thanks to an unhappy, unsympathetic old dentist.

Bob apologized up and down for his behavior. Prior to that visit, we'd had no clue; there was no way to know why he was always so rude. He had hidden the truth, as it embarrassed him *more* than the outbreaks he'd routinely suffer (inflict).

An incredible metamorphosis occurred.  From that day on, he tempered his reactions significantly.  He focused his energies in a positive manner, to help himself move beyond his childhood memories. **Perhaps, too, he sensed *our* increased interest in helping him.**  Our effort was concentrated and genuine.  We understood, for the first time, the battle he fought in his mind.  Together, we beat his phobia, and rebuilt more than his oral health – we restored a part of his soul.

Bob moved to Colorado last year.  Every team member misses him.  During his last years in the Boston area, he became one of our most ardent supporters – and a *cherished* patient.

We listen.  But do we really hear?

## What's *Your* Name?

There are some people who just would laugh at this story: "No way. That *couldn't* be true." Sadly, it is a blow-by-blow description of my encounter with the *extreme team!*

It had been a few years since I'd seen my dermatologist (and friend), Dr. Hubbell. He and I used to share thoughts, occasionally, when I first started out in practice and our offices were across the hall from each other.

We'd both moved to bigger, better locations. Each of us had settled into our own buildings, going our separate ways. I needed his advice and called to set up an appointment.

I arrived at his office five minutes early. As I approached the desk, I saw two 'team' members seated on the other side, both facing me. One was involved in a telephone conversation; the other was wearing dictation headphones and appeared to be transcribing medical records.

I stood at the desk, hoping to catch someone's eye; neither employee acknowledged me, though I was standing less than a yard away. They were both busy. Maybe they'd look up in a moment or two.

It struck me as odd that neither would even smile, nor wave.   Couldn't one of them just break that uncomfortable feeling?  I'm *new* here.  I don't know anybody (except the doctor, who's somewhere out back, *hiding*).

Years ago, Zunan wrote the book, <u>Contact, the First Four Minutes</u>.  Neat idea.  I think he should re-title it, <u>Contact, the First Four *Seconds*</u>!  We really don't have much time at all to create the initial and *lasting* first impression.

I stared for a while, **still hoping to initiate the first human contact.**  After at least three minutes in limbo (which seemed more like three *hours*), the one transcribing slid one earphone off, looked my way and finally greeted me.

"Your *name*?"

I really wasn't prepared for all this kindness at once.  I truly *didn't* know what to say.  I know.  Maybe they think if they shower me with kindness, I'll give them a free lecture on *extreme* customer service!  That's coming anyway!

After pondering, I coolly replied, "*Your* name?"  After all, wouldn't you normally introduce yourself to a new guest in your home? Why should this be any different?

She thought about my response, and retorted (slightly agitated), "Your *name, please*."  Ah, I get it.  She figured if she threw in the 'please,' I'd give it up.

Of course by now you can anticipate my comeback. "*Your* name, please." At this point I'd adopted a rather hostile (and totally appropriate) tone.

They didn't know me from Adam; we were total strangers. They'd obviously never read Tom Peters. He writes about the time he returned to a little Bed & Breakfast, *years* between stays, and upon his entrance into the building, he was greeted, "**Welcome *back*, Dr. Peters. It's so good to have you with us again**. We've been looking forward to seeing you."

How'd they do that? It's not brain surgery, nor rocket science: they have a list of guests and their approximate arrival times. The *extreme team* at Dr. Hubbell's office had far more information to go on. They needed only look at their appointment book, to learn my name, and greet me with civility.

I stand 6-foot, two-inches tall, and broad at the shoulders. I began to look *angry*. They had no clue that I was a patient, and an old friend of the doctor. Only weeks before, a terrible multiple murder (several staff, including the receptionist) had taken place at an abortion clinic in Brookline, Massachusetts – roughly ten miles from where *our* stand-off was transpiring.

The one on the phone sensed a problem, and quietly put down the receiver. They both gave me their full undivided attention. "*May* we *help* you?"

"Yes. I'm Dr. Orent. I have an eleven o'clock appointment to see Dr. Hubbell."

The tensions I've described were no less dramatic than I've related. It's mind boggling that two human beings would treat a guest *or* a stranger in this manner.

---

*Extreme* Autopsy

At the Center for Esthetic Dentistry, we invoked The *Ten-foot* Rule, whenever we are within ten feet of any other human being.

The rule is simple. Any time you are within ten feet of another person, acknowledge them. If you *can*, say hello! If not, then at *least* make eye contact, and a friendly gesture with your hand. **Some of the courtesies we take for granted *shouldn't* be taken for granted.**

## What Time Do *You* Close?

There's a psychological phenomenon that occurs at closing time. *Whatever* your business, there's a tendency for the employees to *wind down* at closing time: "It's been a *long* day. Can't *wait* to get out of here."

The *opposite* feelings are going through your *customers'* minds. "I hope they're still open. I fought 45 minutes of expressway traffic to make it before they close. I just have to pick up that present or Tina will be devastated."

Some Nordstrom legends have echoed through so many lecture halls, it's hard to tell which *actually* occurred. But if you've *been* to Nordstrom, you'll appreciate that *any* of them *easily* could be rooted in fact.

One story goes something like this: a young mother headed out, with her daughter, to her daughter's best friend's birthday party. They'd not had a chance to pick up a gift, and were desperate to find something to bring.

They arrived at Nordstrom five minutes after the doors were *locked.* Faces to the glass, they peered inside. A woman came to the door, and unlocked it. They told her their plight. She allowed them in, *escorted* them to the right department, helped complete the sale, and *wrapped* the gift for the party!

Compare that with the following: I was recently witness to an embarrassing moment, which contrasts *sharply* with the Nordstrom approach.

It was Sunday afternoon, 3:45 p.m., Eastern Daylight Time – *accurate* to within a second, set by the radio tone. The kids and I ran from the mall to the Post Office, knowing they'd close at 4:00 p.m.  I wanted an opinion on some labels I'd formatted, which needed to be in the mail on Monday.

At 3:58 p.m. and 30 seconds, we walked through the door.  "Whew! We just made it, with less than two minutes to spare!"

As I walked by the clerk at the front doors, I said (in a very friendly tone)  "Just a minute- thirty left to go!"

He replied, "No, just 30 seconds left."

I said, "Your watch is a bit fast," and walked on.

Another man walked in right in back of me.
"Sir, we're *closed*," barked the clerk.

Apparently, the other customer had done the same with *his* watch (synchronized to the radio tone). He said, "No, there's over a minute left!"

"Sir, *Postal time* is what *we* go by, and we're *closed!*"

Bear in mind that *every* soul in the lobby is listening to this, *including* all the other postal employees, still manning their stations.

"*POSTAL* TIME IS WHAT *WE* GO BY!"

I just cannot stand by while another person is treated like that. "C'mon," I said. "Let the poor guy in. It's not even 4:00!"

"Would *you* like to speak with my *supervisor*?"

"Me?  Not especially.  But why don't you let the guy in?"

This particular Post Office has terrific employees.  It takes only a single individual to destroy the efforts of an entire team.  The supervisor *did* finally come out, and she *did* allow the man to complete his transaction.

On the way out, the gruff one said to me, "If we didn't draw the line *somewhere* we'd be here all night."

---

*Extreme* Autopsy

This one's a no-brainer.  If the employee cared *at all* about his customers, he would never dream of treating anyone that way.

There are two sides to every story.  Perhaps there's a modicum of truth to his statement, "If we didn't draw the line *somewhere,* we'd be here all night."  But the likelihood that a never-ending flow of humanity would beseech his post is ridiculous.

It's truly a no-brainer. At the posted closing time (for goodness sake, make sure your clocks are accurate, if you're going to be a stickler), *be* the "gatekeeper," if you must. *However*, whether you *lock* a door, or *draw* a curtain or *close* a gate, **wait until there's an obvious break** – even if that means staying open 10 minutes longer (I realize I may be preaching to the choir). Cutting off one person – who walked in immediately in back of another – is rude, demeaning, and embarrassing... to say the very *least*.

## What Time Does Your *Kitchen* Close?

Business travel is only glamorous to those who've never done much of it. I love lecturing, meeting new people, and visiting new places, but it *can* be exhausting.

Recently, I was lecturing in Philadelphia. I always try to arrange my travel so that I'm at dinner no later than 9:00 p.m. the night before the seminar. A bit behind schedule, I was just finishing dinner at the Nameless Hotel. It was 10:55 p.m. (*exactly*).

A rather loud conversation caught my attention: the hostess was involved in a shouting match with a patron who wanted to sit down to dinner. It didn't appear that either was particularly interested in maintaining the pleasant atmosphere; rather, it was more of a shouting contest.

"Sir, I'm *sorry*. We're closed."

"What time did you *close*?"

"We closed at *11:00*."

Meanwhile, I checked my watch (as did everyone else within earshot) – it was 10:55 p.m.

"Your clock is *fast*!"

"I'm afraid it's *not*."

"*My* watch is synchronized with the Atomic Clock in Colorado!"

Then the man said a few unsavory words about the hostess and the hotel. A waiter stepped forward, by the receptionist's side, and called hotel security.

Again, it's the closing time story. What time do you close? Is *closing* just a matter of policy? Is there a chef behind the line so big, bad and mean that you can't persuade him to cook for one (or two or three or four...) more parties?

Just the fact that you're reading this book leads me to believe that you are the type who would keep the doors open for the "just-in-time" customer.

If not, do everyone a favor. Set your watch accurately. The only thing worse than denying a patron the opportunity to give you his or her business, based upon your watch, is denying them when your watch is *wrong!*

I was so uncomfortable watching the episode that I had to tell someone: so, the next morning, I related the entire story to the 300 people in my lecture room... in that *very* hotel!

*Extreme* Autopsy

This is an easy one: Aim to *Serve*. If you are in a service industry, and want to excel, then *serve*. If you want 9 to 5, which won't ever be based upon the public's needs and desires, *avoid* service positions. Surprise someone: "Yes, sir, we did close 10 minutes ago. Although the grill has shut down, the chef would be delighted to serve you any sandwich, or a pizza. May I seat you? What may I get you to drink while you decide?"

It's easy to tell whether or not the invitation is sincere. Make every effort to put *yourself* into the weary travelers' shoes. Once you do, your level of commitment to service will reflect the *extreme* that wins customers' hearts every time.

Please revisit the previous chapter, entitled "What Time Do *You* Close?"

## What Time Do *We* Close?

We began our day at 7:00 a.m. It was 7:00 *p.m.* and we were all about ready to split. My dental team puts in very dedicated, long hard hours. It was time to go home.

Just as we said goodnight to the last patient, the intercom rang. The receptionist told me of a man who'd stopped in because he saw our sign. He had an emergency.

John was a 36-year old executive who'd been playing in a men's league basketball game. He went up for a rebound, missed the ball, but *caught* an elbow. According to John, his opponent grabbed the rebound and came down elbows flailing – the way Kareem Abdul Jabar used to!

He was on his way to the Metrowest Medical Center, and noticed our sign. John was holding a bloody cloth over his mouth. It was difficult, at first, to assess the extent of the damage.

So the question is "how late are *we* open?" Sure, you might say, "This is *different,* it is a medical emergency, of sorts. Yes, *but*...our focus was smile design and smile-*makeovers*. We aren't typically involved with cases where the teeth are moving, and the mouth filled with blood.

At 7:00 p.m., faced with this type of traumatic injury, it would have been simpler, *and reasonable*, to have sent him to the hospital. The Medical Center is only two minutes by car, and they have an oral surgeon on call.

My staff and I agreed to assess the damage, and see if we could handle it. One of his front teeth was 75% knocked out of its socket. Two other teeth were loose, but only slightly. There was still a significant amount of bleeding.

My hygienist, Jim, and my dental assistant, Izabel, both agreed to stay and help do whatever it took to fix him up. We ended up with more than we bargained for.

Initially, we radiographed the area to rule out any jaw fracture, which *would* have necessitated a trip to the ER. He was lucky the bone was intact. But once the bleeding was under control, we could see more clearly: in an area spanning three or four teeth, John's gums had lifted clean off the bone, and were attached only by a small remaining piece. This *was* beyond our usual scope. I told John that while I would be happy to try to help him, it was *not* an injury with which I was experienced. I offered to page a periodontal specialist, if he preferred. It was already 8:00 p.m., and John asked me to do my best to put him back together.

By 10:00 p.m., his teeth were re-implanted, and stabilized with a bonded mesh splint. We had sutured his gums back in place, and he was ready to head home. At my recommendation, John did follow up with a number of visits to my periodontist, and is doing remarkably well.

*Extreme* Autopsy

Compassion is the key.   If someone walks in a moment before you close shop, put yourself in *his* or *her* shoes. Is there *any* way that you can help the customer?

## What Time Do You *Really* Close?

Bob Sage stores his powerboat at the Little River Boat Yard, in Falmouth, Massachusetts. Little River always fills it with gas, and keeps it in good repair. He has a captain for his boat. Between uses, the boat is stored in the boatyard, on racks, accessible by crane.

One lovely summer day, Little River moved the boat into the water, and the captain prepared it for a family outing to Martha's Vineyard. On the way back, **they ran out of gas...in the middle of the Atlantic Ocean!**

They called Little River to tow them back. The one-hour tow home was free because the folks at Little River felt responsible for not having filled the gas tank. Then, because they had inconvenienced their customer, they filled the tank at no charge (unlike a car, boat tanks are enormous and can cost hundreds of dollars to fill).

Great service? Sure. But *here's* the *extreme*... The owner, **Mr. Burdis, offered to store the boat, and do any repairs, for the next year, AT NO CHARGE!**

Mr. Sage was very gracious about the incident, and continued to store his boat at Little River; *however,* he did not accept the offer of free storage and repair. He told the owner that, while he appreciated the offer, Mr. Burdis was running a business, and he wanted to scc the boatyard receive proper compensation.

## Thrifty Angel

It was an unusually hot July. Elizabeth Curran began her California vacation waiting in line for a Thrifty Rental car. It was on that day that she saw an angel.

The Ontario, CA airport had been very busy that particular day and there were lines everywhere one looked. Everything was melting, *including* everyone's patience.

Directly in front of Elizabeth stood an elderly couple. She overheard the problem they were having: they were trying to rent a car to visit their dying brother in the hospital.

Unfortunately, their ages exceeded the upper limits of eligibility for a car's rental. The manager stepped in. In response to their distress, and with a display of incredible compassion, he had a car pulled around. He loaded up the old folks and drove them to the hospital, himself.

## The Bus

Let's take a brief look at 'transportation hierarchy.' What comes to mind when you think of the ultimate in ground transportation for hire?

Chauffeured limousines. A super stretch limo with all the fixings – fully stocked bar, cell phone, television, and an intercom to the driver. The chauffeur takes your bag, opens the door, "Yes, *sir*, ...yes, *ma'am*." You get the picture. What do you think you'd pay for a service like this to take you to the airport, 40 minutes away? For this level of comfort and customer service, you're already in the neighborhood of a couple hundred dollars (or *more,* especially since most services at this level would charge a minimum number of hours).

What's at the opposite end of the spectrum? Public transportation. The *bus*. What comes to mind when you think of the 'city bus?' Crowded, standing room only, dirty, filled with cheap billboard ads and graffiti? A driver who *insists* on the right change, and might kick your mother off if she didn't have the *exact* fare?

You get what you pay for, right? Sometimes. Often you get a little bit less. Sometimes, though, you get a *lot* more.

The following, *extreme* customer service story is *proof* that "government" and "*great* customer service" aren't mutually exclusive.

I live and work in Framingham, Massachusetts. We're about one-half hour west of Boston, and roughly 40 minutes from Logan Airport (unless, of course, Boston's "Big Dig" slows things down, in which case expect delays requiring cryogenics).

Driving yourself *is* an option, but not a great one. First, you have to fight the traffic on the Expressway (ever since I was little, I wondered why Boston calls that road the *Express*way). Then try to find parking. They're working on a 3,000-space addition to Logan Airport's central parking area. Of course, the project is taking just a bit longer than expected, *and* they've lost 50% of the existing parking during construction.

To drive in (tolls and more tolls), park for just two days, and drive home would cost a minimum of $50.00. I realize those of you from New York think I'm crazy to pass up such a great deal – once a friend and I pulled into a Manhattan garage, and they requested a $50.00 cash *deposit*! And we weren't even sure the guy was *employed* there!

Of course taxicabs are an option. Door to door, at *your* convenience. The cab from Framingham, *with* a tip, is $60.00 each way. But if you enjoy a thrill ride, it's a *fare* fee!

So what about the bus? Picture this: Massport Authority, the governmental body in charge of moving people from here to there, had a neat idea that would decrease Expressway congestion (unclog the artery, as they say on the traffic reports), and lighten the airport parking load.

How'd they *do* that?  "Logan Express," a system of buses which run round trips between Boston's Logan Airport and five surrounding communities.  To my glee, *Framingham* is the Western suburban site; the others are scattered in a ring surrounding Boston.  All are roughly 45 minutes out, in average traffic.

Massport designed and built brand new mini-terminal buildings for each of the routes.  Framingham's station seats about 40 people very comfortably.  The station is brightly lit, and tastefully decorated.  There are public facilities, as well as payphones and an array of vending machines.

Cabs are available to and from the Logan Express Bus terminal, and there is ample parking for just $6.00 per day.  The Logan Express bus service runs from 4:30 a.m. to midnight weekdays, and 6:00 a.m. to midnight on the weekends, 365 days a year. On peak, buses run every 30 minutes to and from the airport, to each location.  Off-peak buses are on the hour.

So where's the sacrifice?  How are the actual *buses* and the *service*?  Massport purchased *brand-new* luxury liner buses, each equipped with a restroom, a public cell-phone, and plush, roomy seating *far* more comfortable than the airline seats they're taking you to.

And they are the most prompt service I've ever seen. If you want to set your watch to the second, just mark the time as the bus leaves the terminal.  They're keenly aware that airport goers are travelling on a schedule.

The ride is smooth and quiet.  Once underway, a recording tells you all about your trip.  "Welcome to the Framingham Logan Express.  Your ride to the airport should take approximately 40 minutes, traffic permitting. The driver will be checking in with "Smart Routes" for up-to-the-minute traffic alerts, so that he may get you there as quickly and safely as possible."

I like the fact that the drivers really do check traffic reports constantly (when I drive myself, I usually only remember to check in with the cellular "Smart Routes" service *after* I hit a mess – and then just to find out how badly I screwed up!).

In addition to checking the "Smart Routes" service, Logan Express drivers continuously update each other, as well. Several buses run simultaneously at different stages of the route; at the first sign of congestion, they caution the other drivers and recommend alternate routes.

The drivers make you feel as if you were in that stretch limousine. I've packed some seriously overweight (60 or 70 pounds wouldn't be unusual) and oversized luggage for my seminars. Although I always offer to help them stow the bags, they inevitably insist on handling it for me.

As the Express approaches the airport, the tape plays again, this time announcing the airlines located in each terminal, stop by stop. The drivers are always courteous.

My favorite little service touch (this is truly extreme) is on the ride home. About ten minutes from the Framingham terminal, the driver passes around a blank piece of paper. He then announces over the public address system, "Ladies and gentlemen, thank you for riding the Logan Express, today. If you would like a (sorry!) taxicab waiting for you at the terminal, please use the blank paper to indicate the address of your final destination."

*Unbelievable!* The driver radios ahead to the dispatcher at the terminal, who calls the local Cab Company and tells them how many vehicles are needed and where they will be heading.

So what do they *charge* for this type of service?  We travel in *extreme* comfort, *extremely* promptly, with the most courteous staff one could hope for.  The charge? A one-way ticket on the Express is $8.00 on a weekday and $7.00 on weekends – and seniors take one dollar off all tickets!

You haven't even heard the best part, . If you have, in your possession, a pre-purchased ticket (I *always* buy them in books of ten, and keep a couple in my wallet), you win the deal of the century.

Twenty-four hours a day, there is a Massport authority employee at every airport terminal.  If you arrive at Logan during the hours the Express is shut down, they will accept your ticket and issue a voucher for a taxicab: **your $7.00 ticket** *in exchange for a $50.00 cab ride!* Many times I've arrived at Logan after midnight, *after* the last Logan Express has headed out for the night.  Every cab driver has been nice enough to go the extra mile, and drop me off right at my house.

I've never been so overwhelmingly enthusiastic about *any* other government service. Ever. Massport deserves an abundance of credit for their dream, and subsequent precise and effective implementation.

## Late For Their Meetings

The following story is *not* about customer service, it *is* about human compassion. Compassion and *extreme* customer service are inextricably intertwined. Picture *yourself* caught in Mr. Kravets' shoes...

Howard Kravets was in Tokyo, Japan, on a business trip. He was just learning to speak Japanese, and was not yet fluent. His tutor told him that the *only* way he would gain confidence in his language ability was immersion. He should go out on his own, and try to get around.

He had an important business meeting to attend in Nikko. He would travel by train. He followed some directions to what he had hoped was the Tokyo train station, but Howard arrived at what appeared more like a giant shopping plaza than a train station.

He became concerned that he may have jeopardized the meeting. He had no idea where he was, or how to get to Nikko. A Japanese man was running by, in a *great* hurry, going the opposite way. Howard stopped him, in a most respectful manner, and asked in his newly acquired Japanese, "Where is the train station?"

The gentleman made a sweeping motion with his arms. Apparently, this *was* the train station. Howard asked, "Where are the trains to Nikko?"

The gentleman again made a sweeping gesture. Howard realized that the man wanted him to follow. The man did a 180-degree about-face from his initial direction. Together, they walked about a mile to where the trains departed. There were two white lines painted on the floor.

The train's computerized doors opened. The man motioned for Howard to stand between the two lines: *this* was the boarding area for Nikko!

Howard reached the meeting in time, thanks to a display of *extreme* compassion, by a stranger – a stranger who **compromised his *own* needs for the benefit of another human being in need**.

## Monday, By 6:00 p.m.!

Ma Bell was fragmented years ago – mostly to the benefit of the end users. But occasionally we *suffer* *extreme* examples of service that ought not to be.

Early one *Saturday* morning, my home phone line was dead. There was no dial tone – in fact, there wasn't any noise at all. It was just *dead.*

I used a cell phone to alert the Phone Company of the problem. The repair number was answered by an automated system that *didn't* include the option of speaking to a human being. After punching in various numbers to complete the report, the system told me that my phone should be back in service no later than *Monday* evening, by 6:00 p.m.!

Try as I did, there was no way around the automated system, and I could find no one else to call. **I had no service from Saturday morning, until Monday**, when I called back and spoke to a representative.

He was *very* nice, and **guessed the problem during the first few seconds of my call**. "Sir, do you have any wireless phones on that line?"

"Sure, two of them. Why?"

"Unplug the wireless phones from the line, and wait five minutes."

Sure enough, in a matter of minutes, my phone line had reset itself! Apparently *the* most common cause of line failure is a quirk common to wireless phones. He was right on target, extremely polite, and a pleasure to have on the other end of the line!

Even if they chose *not* to have live support over the weekend (which is beyond my understanding), how could they have improved the situation... *without* investing another penny?

---

*Extreme* Autopsy

After the automated system takes your number, it could add the following menu option: "Thank you for calling repair. Your line should be back in service by 6:00 p.m. on Monday. There are some very simple solutions to the most common problems, which you *may* be able to resolve *yourself*. If you would like to hear a list of the five most common problems, and their remedies, press "2", *now*."

Are there *simple* effective solutions *your* company could offer which require only your thought and some extra effort, *rather* than capital investment?

---

## Staples. And *Much* More.

It's rare that I'm blown away by customer service in a setting as mundane as an office supply store, but it has happened more than once. At the same place and by the same young man. He works at Staples, an office supply *super store*.

Before I tell you about Keith, a few words about the competition. When Staples doesn't have what I'm looking for (which is rare), I visit a competitor. The competition exemplifies typical customer service, American style.

As you enter the store, you may see three or four store employees going about their business. *However,* as soon as you try to locate one of them for help, they're *gone*.

Ready to check out at the register? On many occasions I've reached the register, taking my position as third or fourth in line. Three or four other employees stand near the front, *not one* willing (able?) to open another register.

Compare that with the following. I entered Staples with a short list of items to purchase. The store was moderately busy. One of their associates, Keith Lee, approached me.

"May I help you find anything today, sir?"

"No, that's okay. But thanks anyway." I thought about it for a moment. Why not take advantage of his offer? "On second thought, sure. I'm looking for laser labels for name badges."

"Come right this way." What a refreshing change from the typical department store answer, e.g., "Sure, we've got those. Follow the signs for printing supplies. Go all the way down to the far-left corner of the store. Come back up two aisles, then turn right where it says…"

Keith walked me over to the section with the laser labels. He helped me determine which label best suited my needs, then *he* placed the box into my basket.

"What else, sir?"

I read off the next item from the list. Item by item he accompanied me, made suggestions, as appropriate, and then placed them into my basket. He'd become my 'personal shopper.'

When I finished, he walked me to an open register (they had more registers open than needed, and, subsequently, no lines). He asked the register clerk to take good care of me.

Then, the register clerk asked, "Did you find everything you needed, today?" What a *great* question. So simple, yet a nice courtesy. And, of course, if there *were* something I couldn't find, they were right there to correct that.

On another occasion I needed a refill for a Mont Blanc pen. Keith was waiting for me at the door (I didn't even have a reservation!). He escorted me to the pen counter.

I told him that I didn't want the same type of cartridge I'd had in the past; I wanted to try something different, but wasn't sure of my options.

What could be *extreme* about this experience? **Keith ripped open six different packages** and let me *try each* type of cartridge in my pen! When I was satisfied, *he* was happy.

Often it's the silliest little details that delight the customer most. If my customer were a guest in my home, I would...

"WHEN *I* WAS HAPPY, *HE* WAS HAPPY"

## It's *Only* Ninety Cents

Did you ever see that news magazine piece about the checkout scanners? If *not*, consider this your warning: read *every* item on your grocery receipt. The high percentage of errors is *ghastly*.

If you've not yet made a habit of checking the scanner's accuracy, you have *no* idea what you've been missing. Last night, I was at one of those grocery 'super stores.' I only stopped for two 'quick' items.

It wasn't to be! It took me all of about two minutes to choose a dozen eggs and a package of Mozzarella cheese. It was five minutes 'till closing time (okay, you'd think I'd learn – maybe I *like* living on the edge).

This particular store has 21 checkout registers: only *one* was open. There were at least four employees nearby, very busily making sure they'd be out on time. I glared at one from the distance, hoping to persuade him to open another register.

I stood with my two items, in back of a woman preparing for Hurricane Andrew. It brought to mind the old George Carlin line, "Pardon me, would you mind if I cut in front of you... I only have a *full* cart!" So I waited. Patiently. Really.

My turn. The young lady who checked me out told me it was her first night. No kidding. She *was* very pleasant, and will do well, with some practice. In fact, I think she already had that scanner trick down... two items, one scanned wrong.  Let's see.  That's 50% accuracy!

I didn't notice the scanning error until after I'd paid and she had started serving the next customer.  The cheese was marked $3.39, but it rang in at $4.29.  To refund or not to refund?  Was it really worth the extra time it would take to have someone enter DEFCON1 security codes into Parkway's register?  All for *only* 90 cents?

Sure.  **It was worth it on principle alone.**  There are so many scanning errors that we *can't* just let them go. The supervisor placed her security key into the register, and entered a 62 digits-long code.  Voila!

I was actually pleasantly surprised, when she handed me $4.29 instead of $.90.  She told me I was due a full refund.  Excellent policy.  It was worth the wait, and handled very nicely.

## It's *Only* Forty Cents

At lunch, soup is a regular thing for me. I stopped by my favorite yuppie soup shop, ready to savor the fare. The Lobster Bisque looked especially inviting. I ordered my bisque and picked up a bag of chips.

I noticed that the bag of chips was only half the usual size. It seemed as if there'd be barely *any* chips in it. I checked the label: sure enough, one-half ounce. Their usual bag (still only a tease) was one ounce.

I grabbed a second bag. "Where are your usual chips?"

"Those *are* the usual chips."

"Nope. They're only a half-ounce." *Never* argue weights and measures with anyone who synchronizes their watch to the Atomic Clock in Colorado! That's okay. I'll just take two bags."

"I didn't even notice they'd left those. The salesman must have goofed."

The shop uses the kind of register that has the name of each item on a separate key. All the codes and prices are entered ahead. So I asked, "How will you enter two half-ounce bags?"

"I'll just charge you for *one* of them."

"Great idea." That was that, or so I thought at the time. I returned to my haunt again, about a week later. The 'salesman' hadn't corrected the chips 'error' yet: still a bunch of half-ounce bags.

"Do you know if they've adjusted the codes in the computer for the half-sized bags yet?"

"I'm sure the manager must have taken care of that by now."

I looked at my receipt. I was charged for two one-ounce bags. Big deal, it's only 40 cents right? It *is* a big deal. **Too many folks in service-America say what customers want to hear, but do whatever's most convenient for them.**

I pointed out the discrepancy, again. "Oh. Sorry, they must not have fixed that yet. The salesman is supposed to bring us the regular chips soon, anyway."

Another week went by: same chips, same results. Again they adjust the total *after* I complain. It's by no means the 40 cents – it's the principle behind them intentionally (or otherwise) ignoring the situation and **overcharging *every* customer who bought chips, for three weeks running**.

---

*Extreme* Autopsy

This situation calls for a look at two different, but equally important principles: e*thics* and *follow-up*. Let's give them the benefit of the doubt – I'd hate to think *otherwise*, as it would imply intentional deception.

More likely, it's simply a matter of poor follow-up. Do *you* have a *system* for follow-up? How might this situation have been properly addressed – *not* allowed to fall through the cracks?

The solution might be as simple as a 99-cent spiral-bound notebook. Any time a situation that warrants management attention arises *write it down!* No, it's not rocket science, but the mark of a business that cares.

Of course, in an operation where the staff has access to computers, a note on the company Intranet, or into a network file used specifically for daily follow-up, would be great.

Is it likely that this franchised yuppie soupery has unethical management who is purposely stealing 40 cents from their good customers? Nope. Most likely the management, for three weeks running, never knew a problem existed.

Do you have some 'chips' in *your* business that frustrate the hell out of *your* customers?

## Pass on the Power

It's one of those restaurants where – the moment you walk in – you just *know* it's going to be wonderful. Skip suggested we dine at Sam and Harry's that evening, in Washington, D.C.

The entire experience was one of *extreme* customer service. When you find such a place:

1) It's usually not a secret (*they're packed*)

2) Invisible, predefined systems are followed seamlessly (you never *realize* how much of their manner and motion are rehearsed)

3) The end result is a feeling of luxury and contentment. Patrons *know* they've been treated to a 'Five-Star' experience.

Although the restaurant was packed, our table for six was ready within moments of our arrival. What stands out most, in my mind, was a waitress' ability to turn a potentially negative situation into an *extreme* positive.

They were incredibly busy, and Peggy, Skip's 'usual' waitress, couldn't serve us. Peggy *did,* however, accompany our waitress to the table to introduce her to us personally!

"Mr. Close, I'm afraid I won't be able to serve you this evening. Susan will be your server. I trained her *myself.* **You *will* receive the same excellent attention** you are accustomed to… and I will keep my eye on you, as well."

I was duly impressed. Susan *was,* in fact, outstanding. Peggy 'passed on the power,' so to speak. Skip liked and trusted Peggy. If Peggy says Susan is outstanding, then we are reassured that the evening will be a success.

---

Extreme *Autopsy*

When my receptionist spends time with a new patient, she's sure to show them around and introduce them to the other staff. We're very proud of each and every team member. So when, for example, she's introducing Jim, our hygienist, she might say, "I'd like you to meet Jim. He's our hygienist – **and one of the most *thorough,* yet *gentle* hygienists you'll ever meet. He's *terrific.*"

How can *your staff* "pass on the power?"

## Daddy, Are *We* Homeless?

You'd think that a guy who plans 40 to 50 business trips per year would do better than this on his leisure... I screwed up, big time.

Every summer, I take part in an invitational volleyball tournament in Bartlett, New Hampshire. Players from all over New England meet for this annual two-day friendship tournament.

My 11-year old son, Brendon, grew up with volleyball. He knows many of the summer tournament's participants by name. Between matches, he gets out there on the court *with* us, and helps with the warm-up drills. No wonder he's the best volleyball player in his class!

We'll not soon forget the summer of '98. From Boston, Bartlett is a bit more than a three-hour drive. Usually we drive up the Friday night before the tournament. This particular trip was tough, logistically. I lectured in Biloxi, Mississippi on Friday. My return flight into Boston, plus a bus and one cab ride, put me in bed around 1:00 a.m., Saturday.

We awakened (*barely*) at 5:00 a.m., Saturday, and were on the road by 6:00. I would have *far* preferred to have Brendon drive, but he refused. Said he was only eleven. Traffic was light, the day was gorgeous, and the ride quite pleasant – despite our sleep deprived state.

We arrived at the tournament right on time, at 9:00 a.m. – a small miracle. We had a terrific day together.

Having driven straight to the tournament, I didn't even think to check-in at our motel. At 7:00 p.m., *exhausted*, we headed to dinner.

Seems each year we land at the Red Parka Pub; the food is *always* terrific. By coincidence (though not totally unexpected), we ran into a couple other volleyball families.

We pulled all three tables together, and made an evening of it – literally. Before we realized, it was after 9:00 p.m. There was time to steal enough sleep to play one more day of volleyball and head home.

Now for my big screw-up: I had not confirmed our reservation at the motel. What I thought was a solid reservation was perceived as merely an inquiry. Not to worry – **there have to be about a million rooms in the Mount Washington Valley**. I know the area well; as a teenager, I'd spent my summers there.

We apologized for the misunderstanding, and headed out the door. I told Brendon it shouldn't be a problem finding a nice place to stay. As we drove, we shared our requirements for the 'new' place.

The Valley area is quite spread out, with many quaint little towns dotting the countryside. Jackson, Bartlett, and Glenn were among my favorites. The first few places we tried were full. Not to worry.

Apparently, others had the same favorite spots, and better reservations, as well! We drove on...and on. Many places were kind enough to have their "No Vacancy" signs well lit. Others appeared to have rooms, but we learned that they, too, were full.

At 10:00 p.m., I wasn't "concerned" but I *was* losing consciousness! Four hours sleep between the Biloxi lecture and a full day of volleyball and driving had worn thin. Brendon and I decided to review our individual requirements for lodging. He agreed to drop the need for a game room. I scratched the bed and breakfast.

We drove on. We traveled northwest by Attitash and northeast by Wildcat Mountain. Jackson, Bartlett, Glenn... we were running out of quaint little towns. It had become painfully apparent that I'd chosen a very busy weekend on which to mess up.

I gave in to the notion that I'd have to head into North Conway if we wanted a place to stay. It's a lovely town, just a bit more 'touristy' and congested than the surrounds. By 10:30 p.m., we were cruising in North Conway. But the results were the same: No Vacancy.

Though a bit pricier, I decided we'd try the Red Jacket Inn, which had more rooms than any other hotel or motel in the Valley. I'd stayed there once – perhaps 25 years ago.

We approached the Red Jacket. A majestic structure, it stands way atop a hill, overlooking the Valley below.

A seemingly endless row of lanterns lit the winding way to the top.

Next to the front doors you could see the pool through an immense glass wall. Brendon remarked that the pool looked awesome. "Dad, we should swim." It did look nice. But a bed would look even better.

I approached the registration desk with butterflies in my stomach. The couple in front of us was, apparently, on the same quest for any room in the Valley: it might as well have been for the Holy Grail.

My turn: I sheepishly asked the registration clerk if they had *any* rooms. He apologized, and said they did not. I overheard a man ask one of the clerks, "How many times have you been asked that question tonight?" His answer was scary, "At least a thousand." Of course, his thousand was likely as accurate as my 'million' rooms in the Mount Washington Valley. We just needed *one*.

Brendon was lying down on a couch in the lobby. He was nearly asleep. Caroline, the manager on duty, came over and introduced herself to me. "I'm so sorry. There isn't a single room in the Valley, tonight. We've called around for other guests, and *no* one has *anything* at all."

"Isn't there *anything* you can think of?"

"I wish there were. There's simply *nothing*. It's one of the busiest weekends we've seen this summer."

Terrific: three hours from home, and on less sleep than humane, we had nowhere to sleep. I'll not easily forget what Brendon asked. "Dad, are we homeless?"

It was as good an opportunity as one gets to help instill life perspective.

"No, Brendon, we're not homeless. One way or another we'll find a place, but you know something? The feeling we have now? Tired, and no place to sleep... is something that a lot of people really *do* live with every day of their lives." It's funny how such an innocent question from an 11-year old stirs up emotions, wisdom and sage – in equal parts.

Caroline asked me to wait for a moment, said she'd try a few more places, just in case she'd overlooked anything. I sat next to Brendon, who had drifted off again. As we waited, an endless stream of hopeful patrons made their way to the desk, asking the eternal question, "Any vacancy?"

Caroline came over to us. You could see that she was genuinely disappointed *for* us. "I'm sorry, there really is nothing. If you like, I'll call Waterville Valley or Sunday River, in Maine."

She'd been terrific. At least 20 minutes – and I don't know how many calls – later, **she found the very last room, in Bethel, Maine**. "There's one room left at the Conference Center at Sunday River. Do you want it?"

"What kind of a drive would that be?"

"About an hour and a half."

"Thanks. I guess we don't have a lot of choice at this point."

As if she hadn't gone out of her way enough, **she took my credit card, and made the reservation for me!** She was truly an angel. After she completed the reservation, I spoke briefly to the receptionist at the Conference Center in Maine. She gave me directions, and told me to watch carefully for moose! Ninety minutes of back-road driving, dodging moose!

Caroline was our Angel. Before she'd landed us the room in Maine, I'd thought of turning around and driving home, to Boston. An unbearable thought, as we didn't leave the Red Jacket until 11:00 p.m. (our eventual check in was 1:00 a.m. sharp, in Bethel, Maine)!

I won't wait another 25 years before we stay at the Red Jacket. Our angel had taken *extreme* customer service to heart. She took it upon herself to make certain that we were safe and sound before the dawn broke over the Valley.

## The Cab

As a visitor to Manhattan, have you ever tried to hail a cab? Boston drivers are known throughout the country as aggressive, offensive, and downright rude. But all that great training never prepared me for cab hailing in New York City.

New York is one of my most frequent 'customers.' I presented five New York seminars during one 12-month period. I still need help, though, getting a cab.

When I was 19 years old, I was in a bad car accident that resulted in two fractured vertebrae. As a passenger in that car, there was a terrible feeling of helplessness as we skidded 150 feet sideways – at nearly 60 miles per hour—before the car was torn in two.

Every time I get into a cab (*especially* in Manhattan), I tell the driver about that day 21 years ago. It's not that I have a phobia – no flashbacks, nothing like that. It's simply that most cabbies, *especially* in Manhattan, drive like maniacs. Like a Boston driver on amphetamines.

I remember once hearing a lecturer (Tom Peters, if memory serves me) tell a story about a truly *extreme* cab driver. How could a *cabby* make the *extreme* list (other than *extremely* rude)? It went like this…

"Morning, sir. How are you today?"

"Great, thanks. You?"

"Fine, sir. Thank you."

The cab driver passed a china plate back through a slide window in the bulletproof divider. "Care for some crackers and cheese?"

On the china plate was a neat arrangement of crackers and sliced cheese. Saran wrap was carefully stretched over the assortment, keeping it fresh.

"Coffee?"

"Sure."

"Decaf or regular?"

He's got to be kidding. "Decaf."

"Sir what type of music do you prefer. I've got a wide variety of CDs, from Beethoven to pop."

The cabby then offered a choice between the New York Times and the Wall Street Journal. He asked *how* the customer would like the ride – leisurely, moderate pace, or get to the destination as fast as humanly possible.

At the destination, he handed his business card and explained that he would be delighted to be of service in the future. Simply call his cell number an hour or so ahead, and he would take the reservation personally.

Did anybody get that guy's number?!

## The *Extreme* Dream

In this section, we'll explore a variety of different industries.  In The *Extreme* Dream, I'll create *my* model of *extreme* customer service orientation for each industry example.  My models are, by no means, complete guidelines for each industry: they *are* random thoughts, 'gems' (so to speak) to get you thinking.  If you think I'm *beyond* the edge:

1) Re-read the name of the book
2) Rethink what Drucker meant when he said, "Abandon *everything.*"
3) Re-read the chapter entitled, "The Spa."

This is no longer a world where corporations (or corner boutiques, for that matter) can rely on past performance and market trends.  Some of Tom Peters' choice words describe the business environment best: "Chaos, topsy-turvy."  He's been known to suggest that we adopt the attitude of "raving thunder-lizard evangelists!"

When you read The *Extreme* Dream, it may seem funny; in fact, it may seem almost *impossible.*  But it's *deadly* serious.  Don't get caught up in whether or not *your* business is closely related to the examples you'll read.  It's a *lot* closer than you think.  People want to feel extra special – they want you to make them feel *important.*

## The *Extreme* Dream

### *Part I: At the Restaurant*

I remember dining at a restaurant with a friend from out of town. After we'd finished the meal, and were no longer within earshot of the place, my friend said, "Tom, you know, you ought to be a restaurant *critic*."

To which I replied, "I *am*."

In reality, we *all* are. Regardless of the degree, we *all* have a running critique going all day long. "This place was incredible. That place was lousy. Don't ever go there, they..."

Now think about your customers. If you buy that they are *all* constantly evaluating everything you do, then snap into action! Realize that the very first impression counts – big time. And so does every moment and opportunity thereafter.

So what would be my *dream* restaurant? As you pull up to the restaurant, a valet approaches the car. "Good evening, Mr. Jones, a pleasure to see you again, sir. May I park your car?"

Funny, we're not even inside, and you're already thinking, "*We* can't do this." *Sure,* you can (okay, if your business is a Burger King, there will be some issues – cost to benefit ratios, etc.).

But *how* did the valet know Jones' name?

Take a hint from the world's greatest car salesman, Joe Girard. He outsold every other salesman in the country, before the advent of computers, by maintaining a Rolodex file on every customer he met.

When you valet park the car, jot down the license plate number along with the make, model and color. Keep this information with everything else collected about your patron.

At the end of the evening, when your guest is looking for his car, you might beat him to the punch, "Mr. Jones, I certainly hope everything was most enjoyable this evening. You have the silver Camry, if I recall. I'll have that for you in a jiffy." At the risk of redundancy, *this* is but one more way to make Mr. Jones feel very special.

If your restaurant takes reservations, the *next* time Mr. Jones calls for a reservation, several things come into play. For starters, you might say, "Mr. Jones... Nice to hear from you sir... I see...just the two of you tonight? I have that table by the fireplace that you and Mrs. Jones enjoyed the last time you were here." Keep in mind, it's all on the index card (or better, in a Rolodex file, in the computer).

***Immediately* after being seated, the bread arrives!**
Question: Why do people go to a restaurant?
Answer: They are hungry!

The bread in a restaurant is a *make or break* item. How fast was it delivered? The worst case scenario is when the customer sees other patrons with bread at *their* tables, and has to *ask* if his party can have bread, too!

Is it warm? If you don't already serve warm bread, try this experiment. Warm some bread. Put it in a nice wicker basket, with a pretty cloth over the top to retain moisture and heat. Watch folks as they pull back the cloth... the steam rises. They put their faces right over the basket to capture the aroma.

Now go over to the table. Ask the customers if, in the future, they would prefer cold bread on a china plate or this piping hot bread in the wicker basket again? ...Thought so.

Here's another bread story. I visited a great restaurant in Natick, MA, called "Go Fish." As you sit down, they give you *more* than just bread. They *present* you with a platter upon which you'll find the following: wonderfully seasoned, fresh bread sticks (a meal themselves); three different seasoned oils – one hot, one mildly spiced, but incredibly flavorful, and one with a touch of garlic; and a selection of olives. Two of those and a couple of drinks and I'd be fine!

If you serve cold slices of ordinary bread, cut it out! And remember that one of the most negative ways to start the meal is with iced butter. It simply doesn't make any sense! **Warm the butter, warm the bread**. Give some serious thought to seasoned oils, olives, and any other *extreme* way that *you* can make a difference as we start our meal.

The wait staff at my dream restaurant would borrow a concept from Boston's famous Legal Seafood. When the meal is piping hot and ready to be delivered, the *first* available staff rushes the food to the table. Although you do have your own assigned waitperson, they *share* responsibility for *every* patron. Typically, they'll have two or more staff delivering the food simultaneously.

Who cares the *most*? Typically, the assigned wait staff returns to the table to see how well we're doing. That's great, and it's very important. *But*, in *addition* to the wait staff checking, there's nothing like the manager or *owner* coming by every table and taking a personal interest.

At this point, if you are involved in a fast food restaurant or another, similar industry, you're probably picturing the Ritz Carlton and tossing these ideas aside. **You don't have to be the best in the city to *act* like the best!** At one New England chain, Papa Gino's, managers frequently stop by the tables and inquire about the meal… and Gino's is a "fast food" family restaurant!

**Please don't charge for soft-drink refills**. I *know,* you've already figured out that you can make an extra dollar's profit for every second soda. If so, you've truly missed the big picture for two reasons:

1) It's perceived by the public as 'nickel and dime-ing.'
2) Many of your competitors have already decided *not* to charge. You *can't* win if you charge. The actual cost to you for that second soft drink is minimal. The goodwill is large.

Possibly the most delicate timing is the period after the meal is complete. Except at ultra-leisurely establishments (read very expensive)**, staff should facilitate the guests' departure**. A great experience can be dampened by waiting too long to get the check, or change.

And for goodness sake, **please *don't* ask, "Would you like change?"** It's a dead giveaway that you're out of your league. *Instead*, simply say, "Thank you, sir. I'll be back presently with your change." If the patron requires no change, it's up to *them* to say so, if they choose. Please, *don't* ask!

The Extreme Dream

## *Part II: The Airlines*

What's the difference between a herd of sheep and a planeload of travelers? I don't know either.

Doesn't it feel that way? Often? Welcome to my *extreme* dream airlines, where the first motto you encounter is 'cross train.'

Travelers know that the start of every trip includes a potentially long wait in line, to check in and tag your baggage.

Why crosstrain? It's easy for the airlines to know just when they'll need more line agents for check-in. The *tough* part is not overstaffing for all the times between flights, when demand is lower.

By crosstraining, other non-critical personnel could be diverted to the check-in counter. Once the crush is over, they go back to their respective positions. I've seen great examples of this at some of the smaller airports. The most extreme was almost comical:

I landed at an airport in the Midwest. I was the *only* person in the terminal! No other patrons, no staff. As I stepped off the plane, the flight attendant went to the rear of the aircraft and removed my bag. As I stepped onto the runway, I headed toward the rear of the plane, to take the bag from her.

She motioned me away from the luggage and pointed towards the terminal door. Once inside, I watched her pop my bag through a little door in the wall, then run around to the other side, retrieve it, and hand it to me! She was flight attendant, baggage handler, customer service representative – and darned good at *all* of the above.

I realize there's very little room in the jet aisles, that a food and drink cart barely makes it by the seats. It *never* makes it by my elbows! **If you *must* nail my elbows, *at least* apologize!** Sure, you'll need to do a lot of apologizing, but what the heck?

If *your* airline delayed the flight and caused the delays, *you* **call ahead and hold the connections!** In the "old days," they used to hold connections – if it was within the realm of reason. Obviously, if one passenger is going to be two hours late, then holding the flight is absurd – but I was one of 15 passengers who missed a same-airline connection by five minutes!

The airlines have a terribly difficult job to do, and literally *all* the forces of nature working against them. I give them credit for even *wanting* to be in such a challenging industry. Still, be nice, and make us feel special. You, Mr. Airline, *can* do it.

The following anecdote was *not* a dream. It occurred when Northwest airline's pilots were on strike. Well before anyone knew of the potential strike, my travel agent, Fran, booked me on Northwest, Boston to Kansas City, Missouri.

As the seminar date grew closer, I contacted Fran to find out how the strike might affect my plans.

Northwest was canceling flights only two days ahead. The industry had raised their collective consciousness and prepared for travelers booking duplicate itineraries for backup.

Fran advised that there was little that we could do at the time, other than wait and watch. Were we to arrange duplicate routing on a different airline, we could jeopardize the trip, as the airlines might cancel *both* tickets.

Two days before the trip, the pilots were still out, and Northwest began to move ticket holders onto other airlines. It was havoc to the system, trying to accommodate all the displaced passengers from a major airline.

I arrived at Boston's Logan Airport 90 minutes before my re-accommodated flight. I'd been moved to US Air. The airport was a mob scene: there was a long snaking line at the ticket and baggage check-in counter, as one might have expected.

Fran told me to bring the original Northwest tickets to the US Air counter. New tickets were to be issued by the accommodating airlines. Normally, I'd give my bags to the skycaps for curbside check-in; however, without a US Air ticket, I headed inside. I entered the queue, bags in trail.

**I had that uncomfortable feeling that I may wait in the line for a long time... and then find out that it**

**wasn't even the *right* line.** With the mass of travelers, and confusion in general, I didn't want to waste precious time going nowhere.

Not a minute passed before I noticed a uniformed US Air agent walking the queue. He was wearing a two-way radio through which he was patched into the overhead loudspeaker system. Loud and clear, I heard, "Folks, if you are looking for the US Air Shuttle to LaGuardia, you're in the wrong terminal. If so, please step forward and I'll assist you with directions."

"If you have a ticket and a confirmed seat, but no bags, you are welcome to proceed directly to your gate for check-in. If you have a ticket and a confirmed seat, and *do* require baggage check, you may want to use our skycap service for curbside check-in. There are presently only three people waiting in the skycap's line.

"If you are on the 4:57 p.m. flight to Chicago, they are boarding at this time. Please step forward. We will form two lines at the front, alternating you with every other passenger in the main queue."

He was set up with the technology, the authority, and the *desire* to make a difference. I've never felt as comfortable waiting in a long line as I did that day. US Air gets kudos for *extreme* service at a very difficult time for all involved.

## The *Extreme* Dream

### *Part III: Technical Support*

Kudos to those few Technical Support department chiefs who've already pinpointed one of the main frustrations we (the public) experience: *waiting* in queue!

My dream telephone support line would steal the opening line from the fewandfarbetween chiefs who've addressed the queue problem. 'Thank you for calling XYZ Corporation Technical Support line. Our 'time engineering' software has estimated that you will reach an operator in less than four minutes."

Disney is famous for exactly this concept. They know how many people fit into their queues (corrals). They've timed how long it takes to arrive at the ride from various spots in the line. Armed with this knowledge, they place signs along the way: "You are only 30 minutes from the thrill of Space Mountain." A trip to Disney is a great study in *extreme*ly great customer service.

Note that they play a little psychological trick here. If they *know* that it will be 25 minutes from this point, the sign will say 30, or even 35. It's a concept I call *under-promise and over-deliver.* **Tell me the wait at your restaurant will be 45 minutes. Seat me in 35 and I'm yours for life** (well, it's a start).

How can *your staff* 'pass on the power?'

---

*Extreme* Autopsy

**Why** don't most organizations **under-promise and over-deliver?** 'Cause it's a bit scary. We risk losing the customers' business, if they perceive too low a value in the service, based upon your (conservative) description.

Practice the concept, and the world will be yours. If you could **regularly come through for your customers, with slightly more than they anticipated** was possible, you'd be a hero.

---

Back to the queue. Time analysis software can easily determine the average time spent on technical support calls for any given software or department. Of course, the larger your support staff, the more closely statistical averaging will approximate the reality of the next caller's wait.

If you have only five support personnel answering calls, there's a pretty good chance that one unusually long call will skew the numbers (20% of your support team will be delayed far longer than the statistical average). Conversely, if you have 500 operators, the automated estimates should be right on target. Just remember to tweak them a bit in the *under-promise* direction.

In exactly three minutes and thirty seconds (one-half minute before they'd promised) you hear, "Good morning, thanks for calling XYZ Technical Support. This is Sean; how may I help you today?"

Not only did Sean pick up before I expected; he answered in a warm and caring manner. So far he hasn't made me feel like an idiot for not knowing the answer to my own question! **Extremely insensitive technical support personnel tend to make the lay public feel stupid.** That's *hardly* exceeding anyone's expectations for great customer service! Nope. We want to feel *important*.

One of the most brilliant minds in dental software programming is *also* one of the most service oriented and satisfaction savvy – Brian Smith. He wrote Practice Works – a program several years ahead of its time.

In the early 1990s, dental software companies were beginning to offer computerized appointment schedulers. Those dinosaurs looked absolutely *nothing* like the doctor's real appointment book. In fact, they looked more like a top-secret government coding for nuclear retaliation, a code not meant to be cracked or understood by *anyone*!

I remember one trade show vendor trying to convince me that it was time to move into computerized appointment scheduling. "Doctor, this system will *change* the face of your practice."

I looked at the monitor. "What are all those X's and Y's?"

"They *represent* the procedure you'll be doing for that patient."

"What's the eight digit number after the X's and Y's?"

"Those are codings that represent various procedures you do in the office."

"How do you tell how..."

This went on for about five minutes, after which I was convinced that I'd *never* ever allow a computer vendor to mess with my appointment book! It was *frightening*.

My favorite part of that conversation was the last part: "This doesn't look anything like an appointment book. Can't you make it look like my appointment book?"

**"Doctor, *this* is how it *has* to look. You and your staff will eventually get used to it."**

Don't think so. I had one very brave friend who *did* purchase the scheduling component of his software package. I distinctly remember being *shocked* when he told me that they were running *dual* systems for over six months. **Although they had the computer scheduler up and running, they maintained the paper appointment book, as well, for *six* months!**

Brian Smith (with, of course, the advantage of the Windows graphical interface) created a program (<u>Practice Works</u>) that focused *first* on the scheduler. His priority was to **design a software application that resembled the doctor's *already* existing appointment book**, and would be customizable to each practice.

Brian achieved *exactly* that. His program defaults to the scheduler. Doctors using his system put a monitor in every treatment room, as well as in the business and reception areas. At the Center for Aesthetic Dentistry, we now have a live, up-to-the-minute appointment book pasted (electronically) on the face of each monitor! In fact, it's actually *far easier* to work with <u>Practice Works</u>' scheduler than with the old paper systems.

Back to the *Extreme* Dream technical support. We don't need/want to feel like idiots. Brian Smith put it eloquently. He said, **"I take each and every call to the Support line as my own personal failure."** *Imagine* the genius programmer taking the tact that support calls represent failures on *his* end?

I once had a software company executive point out that my office ranked among the top in number of calls to his company's support line. He wasn't passing out an award, though! He suggested we consider purchasing additional training, as it was clear to him that my staff just didn't "get it!" He never considered that a) we might be utilizing features beyond the basics, features that other offices don't even realize exist; or, b) each of our calls was *their* failure!

The *Extreme* Dream Support department should be able to assist the more difficult problems *without* stressing the user's time or limited knowledge. If there are files or changes required that go beyond a few simple keystrokes, figure out a way that *Support* can do the entire fix, without tying up (confusing, and frustrating) the user on the end of the line.

After all, picture going to your neighborhood car mechanic with an engine problem. The mechanic says, **"Mrs. Kraft, why don't you come around the front end here, and hold this screwdriver against this valve for me.** While you give this stem a quarter rotation at a time, I'll..." Of course, it's absurd!

---

*Extreme* Autopsy

If the XYZ Company tech can talk you through some easy keystrokes, great. Otherwise, figure out a way to take the user out of the loop. Free her to do her job, while you do yours by yourself. How? Connect, via modem, directly into the caller's system (use PC Anywhere, for example). Access via the Internet, etc. With today's technology, the *how* is easily accomplished If you want to make the effort to stand out above the crowd.

---

Another most frustrating experience is when the on-line support folks *can't* solve the problem. "I'm sorry, Mr. White, but the problem *isn't* something that can be corrected from this end." This translates into, "I don't know *who* would know all the intricacies of our software and *your* network well enough to help... *but* if that person existed, you should call *them*!"

The *Extreme* Dream Support team has an answer to that. **It's like a computer S.W.A.T. team. Ready to deploy to any part of the nation, overnight**, they arrive at your site, and camp out until the problem is resolved. If your company isn't able to employ this type of a team, full-time, then *outsource* it.

I had the *extremely* great fortune of meeting one of these folks. No one had been able to debug our system. There were random crashes throughout the network. You couldn't be on any computer for more than an hour without it going down. Camera capture took 20 seconds per shot: capture is *supposed* to be almost instantaneous. The list of problems associated with the instability of our network was endless.

The company hired a sort of S.W.A.T. team specialist named Jerry Sladkey. Jerry works with a six-person team of troubleshooters who fly anywhere in the country and *solve* unsolvable problems.

Jerry flew from Southern California to Boston the next night. He set up camp at a local Motel 6, and worked on the system for seven days straight! When Jerry left, the system *sang!* Crashes were eliminated (the next serious episode was almost a year later, and unrelated). Camera capture was *instantaneous*, and all the other little associated bugs disappeared.

---

*Extreme* Autopsy
Does your company have an overnight emergency deployment team? Can you at least recommend one?

---

What a terrific (lifesaving) service to have at your disposal.

# The *Extreme* Dream

## *Part IV: The Gas Station*

Are you old enough to remember what 'full service' used to mean? I have to laugh to myself when I drive into today's filling stations, and see the sign, 'full service.'

Part of my *Extreme* Dream filling station is based, in part, upon childhood memories of what Texaco used to call "Red Ball Service." The "man who wears the star" (the station attendant, not the local law enforcement) would always treat you to the *full* service experience.

I have a clear picture in my mind of an attendant named Tom. He must have been in his fifties when I was a child. Tom would *greet* us. What a great start. The dream station attendant should *greet* the customer!

Tom would ask my mom to lift the hood –at *every* visit. He would routinely check the following: the battery water levels; radiator water/antifreeze levels (unless we'd been driving for a while, and the temperature too high); the oil; and he would *eyeball* the belts, reassuring us that everything under the hood was in tip-top shape.

Today, you'd have to make an appointment for the type of service Tom would offer with every fill – and you'd pay a significant fee for what he believed was just part of his job. But it didn't stop there.

He'd then grab a squeegee and clean the windows. *Not* just the front windshield, all the car's windows! He wasn't caring for the car as much as he *was* servicing the folks inside.

My dream station would do all of the above and *then* some. They'd offer to check the tires. If one were low, they'd have you pull over to the air line after filling the tank. Then (of course) they'd properly inflate your tire.

---

*Extreme* Autopsy

Did today's stations consider the impact of that 25-cent tire air box they installed... did they think beyond the short-term bottom line? Sure, they can rack up a few dollars a day. In a year, that's going to add up to hundreds, or maybe a thousand... get the point? Hundreds, if not thousands, of great customers develop less than extremely warm fuzzies about the station. Whether they ever need air or not.

Do you have 25-cent air pumps in your business?

---

## *Extreme* Consistency

Libertyville Illinois' Pauly Honda will *always* have a special place in Maria Bobrow's heart. Why such a soft spot for a *car* agency? Pauly is famous for *great* customer service... with a simple twist.

Whenever Maria visits Pauly Honda for an oil change, she receives a warm greeting, and is escorted personally to the reception area, where she enjoys choosing from a wide selection of teas and coffees.

Their service is prompt. Repairs *stay* fixed, and folks are always delighted. **The visit always ends with the presentation of a single red rose.**

The twist? Maria has received this level of service, *consistently*, **for almost *ten* years!** Great customer service qualifies as *extreme* when sustained for extensive periods of time.

## In the Land of the *Blinds*

Danny Bobrow ordered custom blinds for his new home. He was told initially that there would be no charge for on-site measurements and an estimate. The company subsequently charged him $39 for on site measurements.

When he ordered the blinds, the manufacturer said they would ship within three weeks. When he asked if they would call when the blinds shipped -- so he could schedule an installation appointment -- he was told that "was not their policy." He would have to wait until the blinds were *delivered* before scheduling an appointment for installation, effectively adding another two-week delay!

The blinds were incorrectly shipped to his home instead of his office. Repeated attempts to reach the company by telephone produced nothing but busy signals. When he finally reached someone, he was advised that **"When things get busy, we take the phone off the hook!"** The company never uses an answering service or an answering machine. And it is a national chain!

Danny asked for assistance in correcting the delivery address, but was told to do it himself. Then the blinds arrived – cut incorrectly, and in a style without a draw wand. He called and cancelled the order.

The manufacturer protested the cancellation to their credit card processing bank. Because the product was 'customized,' the credit card Company sided with the manufacturer, and insisted that Danny pay for the merchandise!

---

*Extreme* Autopsy

Wow! I can't imagine a worse experience trying to get blinds! The common thread? Again it comes down to caring. Not one of the absurdities suffered by Mr. Bobrow would have gone uncorrected... if the company had a heart!

The 'right' things to do are *so* obvious in this case they don't even warrant mention in the autopsy. **And *shame* on the credit card Company** for not digging deep enough to realize the multiple injustices done by *their* merchant to the consumer.

---

"WHEN THINGS GET BUSY, WE TAKE THE PHONE OFF THE HOOK..."

## Satisfaction *Guaranteed*

The following story, told by my mother, Daisy Orent, represents good, old-fashioned customer service. Today, it qualifies to be called extreme customer service!

When Dad and I were engaged, I bought a "smoking jacket" for him at Rogers Peet in Boston; the old standard, maroon corduroy with a black velvet collar. (I, obviously, was fantasizing about our life style.) He kept it in his closet -- with the original stitching closing the pockets, inside a plastic garment bag —for *years*.

One day, my Father and I were in Rogers Peet, and my Dad was buying a suit. I explained to the salesman, that this jacket had hung unused, in Dad's closet for such a long time. **"Bring it back," he said, "and we will give you full credit for it, no matter when you bought it."** We did return it, and they graciously refunded the full purchase price!!!

No wonder that my Dad had been a very satisfied Rogers Peet customer.

## The "Bride"

Legal Seafood has long been known for delicious seafood, as well as great customer service. One evening, one of their restaurants was host to a special anniversary party – a *50th*.

The 'bride' was upset that she had lost her corsage during the evening. The hostess overheard the conversation and took it upon herself to go the extra mile.

During the dinner party, the hostess drove to a local florist and bought a corsage. She presented the new corsage to the 'bride.'

Often, *extreme* customer service involves a simple gesture that speaks volumes to understanding and tending to other folks' happiness.

## Legal Tender

"Legal" stories remind me of Nordstrom.  You wish every establishment would try even *half* as hard to satisfy and fulfill their customers.

An adult son took his father to a Legal Seafood establishment for dinner. The father had Alzheimer's disease. After a fine dinner, the son couldn't find the keys to his car and, during the search, the father became agitated.

The hostess, in a display of *extreme* customer service, gave her personal car keys to the son!  She told him to take his father home, and then return her car later.  The tender manner in which the Legal hostess solved the problem is *exemplary* of 'extreme.'

## Far Away from Home

Boston is host to a number of world-class hospitals, like the Massachusetts General Hospital, Tufts New England Medical Center, The Massachusetts Eye and Ear, and the Brigham and Women's, just to name a few.

People travel from all around the country (and around the world) to take advantage of these hospitals' expertise. When severe illness or injury strikes, more than just the infirmed individuals are affected. Loved ones suffer, as well.

In close proximity to a number of these Boston hospitals is a Howard Johnson's Hotel. Families visiting their hospitalized loved ones often stay at the Howard Johnson's.

The hotel's general manager has made it a personal mission to watch out for this particular type of visitor. He watches especially to see if they are travelling alone. When he finds a family member who has made the trip alone, he offers a compassionate ear.

When his guest returns alone at night from the hospital, he offers to sit with them over coffee. He offers his company, and a listening ear, if they want to talk about the illness. What a wonderful gesture, offering such compassion to those alone in a strange city in their times of desperate need.

## *Extreme* **Personal**

Howard Kravets keeps his 26' powerboat at the marina at Admiral's Cove, in Jupiter, Florida. His boat had been refinished a few hours north of there, and was due for return delivery in the early afternoon.

The boat yard usually closed at four p.m.. At quarter to four, the captain called Mr. Kravets, and said that he was still en route, and would be another hour or so. Howard spoke to the owner of the boatyard, who offered to wait another hour for the boat. Upon arrival, it would have to go, by forklift, onto the storage racks.

Near five o'clock, the captain called again, to say he would arrive about seven p.m.. Howard called the owner, who was leaving for dinner. He gave Howard the telephone number for the restaurant where he and his wife would be dining, and told him to call when the captain arrived with the boat.

The captain **finally pulled in at ten p.m., long after the forklift driver had gone home and the yard officially closed**.

True to his word, the owner returned to help. He couldn't get the lift under the boat until he got down on the ground and unscrewed the license plate, which was in the way. He then operated the lift himself, and put the boat on the rack, for storage.

Howard said, "Whatever you choose to charge me for all of this, will be fine. I am most appreciative of the way you extended yourself for me."

The owner replied, "It was my pleasure to help out. There'll be *NO CHARGE!*"

## *Beyond* the *Job* Description

Michael is a United States Postal Carrier in Newton, Massachusetts.  Mrs. Wheeler was an elderly woman on Michael's route, living alone in a big, old house.

Over the years, Michael offered to help Mrs. Wheeler with the some of the little things that an elderly woman can't easily manage.  He would bring out the trash, on occasion.  If New England weather made the walk dangerous, he'd bring in the newspaper with the mail.

Occasionally, Mrs. Wheeler would ask for assistance with other odds and ends. He gladly did these things as he went about the business of delivering the daily mail.

One day, he heard that she had died. Michael attended her wake, in his Postal uniform.  Only one other man was there.  Michael assumed he was the undertaker.

The man approached Michael, and asked if he had been Mrs. Wheeler's mail carrier. Michael introduced himself.   The man, Mrs. Wheeler's attorney, told Michael that he had been mentioned in her Will;  she was appreciative of the friendliness he had shown and the help he had given .

The attorney explained that Mrs. Wheeler had no family.   With the exception of what she left for Michael, all the rest went to her favorite charities. Michael was left, tax *free,* $100,000.00!

*Extreme* Autopsy

This example of *extreme* customer service was borne out of human kindness – compassion for another's circumstance. It was borne out of the purest of intention – with *absolutely no expectation* of gain or reward.

## "Guaranteed" Late Reservation

What does 'guaranteed late reservation' mean to you? As a very frequent traveler, it's an *essential* comfort for me to know that, *regardless* of my hour of arrival, I have a pillow on which to rest my head.

Dr. Stewart Rosenberg was slated as the keynote speaker for the Texas Academy of Laser Dentistry. He arrived at the Four Seasons, Los Calinas, very late the night before the meeting. At the registration desk, Dr. Rosenberg was informed that his room was unavailable.

Although he had 'guaranteed' late arrival, there was a circumstance beyond the control of the hotel management; a large group, slated to leave the night before, had decided to stay one extra night. By law, the hotel is not allowed to displace a current guest.

Dr. Rosenberg was road weary and visibly upset. The manager was empathetic, and more important, he took *extreme* action. A Four Seasons limousine delivered Dr. Rosenberg and his wife to a nearby hotel. The Four Seasons arranged and paid for their room at the other hotel.

At sunrise, Dr. Rosenberg was delivered, by limo, back to the Four Seasons for his speech. His wife was told to call the Four Seasons when she was ready to return.

At the end of the seminar, Dr. and Mrs. Rosenberg were escorted to their new room at the Four Seasons.

They found two boxes sitting on the bed, beautifully gift-wrapped and adorned with large ribbons. The smaller box had Mrs. Rosenberg's name on it. Inside was a gift certificate for $100.00 to the Four Seasons Spa.

Inside Dr. Rosenberg's box was a stunning Four Seasons golf shirt, and a note:

Dear Dr. and Mrs. Rosenberg:
Please accept these small tokens of our appreciation for your understanding and patience. We sincerely regret the inconvenience you've endured, and hope that we can make the rest of your stay as carefree as possible.

We hope that your meeting was successful. Enjoy the remainder of your days with us. Your *entire* stay will be compliments of the Four Seasons.

Extreme? Certainly. But *that's* the service orientation with which the Four Seasons developed their incredible reputation, one guest at a time.

## A *Thirst* for Customer Service

I flew from Boston to Calgary to present a seminar the following morning. The flight had left me parched and it was very late. When I arrived at the Westin, I headed straight for my room.

Lips, cheek and tongue had become one indistinguishable mass. I decided to grab a Diet Coke. Shoes already off for the night, I headed down the hall in my stocking feet, in search of Diet Coke (unaware that my goal was no less lofty than the Holy Grail itself).

I followed the chatter of the ice machine, certain to find vending nearby. It was an eternity down the long halls. I finally reached the source of the noise: a lone ice machine, *without* its vending companion. There was a sign on the machine, "Soda machines are located on floors 10 and 2."

I ventured to the elevator (no shoes), and journeyed down to the 10th floor. I was borderline on having thirst hallucinations! I found the soda machine. Either it didn't like U.S. coins, or it was out of Diet Coke. I never did figure it out.

Once on the elevator again, I forgot which floor hosted the other machine. I headed to the front desk, figuring for sure there'd be machines somewhere near the lobby.

A young man, John, came to the desk, asking how he could be of service. When I told him of my quest for a Diet Coke, he informed me that the second floor would be the closest place I could try.

Back to the elevator. The second floor machine, was, *of course,* out of Diet Coke! I rode *my* elevator back to the lobby to see John once again. When I told him about my parching flight from Boston, and the subsequent journey through the Westin, he *snapped* into action.

"Sir, I am *so* sorry for your inconvenience. If you could wait here, I'll be back in a moment." John *ran* around to the end of the registration counter, by me, down a short flight of stairs, and disappeared through double doors.

I had no idea where he was headed, but based upon the speed he ran and the five minutes it took him to return, my best guess is that he left the building! Five minutes later, he reappeared, *still* running, a Diet Coke in each hand.

He apologized profusely for my inconvenience, and handed me the icy cold bounty. He refused any sort of repayment *or gratuity* for the drinks. I thanked him and with the Diet Cokes, began one final very early morning elevator journey.

## The Clothes *Make* the Man

Remember <u>Dress for Success</u>, a best seller in the early 1990's? I was to speak before 300 dentists in Wichita, Kansas. In all my travels I'd never lost luggage – until that day.

I arrived at the airport minus my clothes! Denim jeans and a golf shirt were my flight apparel... and the *only* clothes I had in Kansas. I told my seminar host about the predicament; the airlines had a 'watch' out for my bag, and promised to deliver it post-haste to the hotel... when it was recovered.

The meeting was to start at 8:00 a.m. No time to wait for the stores to open – let alone shop for a new suit! I was already contemplating standing before the audience asking forgiveness for my attire. *Not* a great way to kick off the meeting!

At 7:15 a.m., my host introduced me to Judy, a stunning young blonde woman, who was the director of catering and functions for the Marriott Hotel.

Judy's opening line shocked me. "Dr. Orent, I understand you arrived last night short one of your bags. You're about the same height and weight as my husband *and* my son. Why don't you come home with me and we'll see if we can outfit you for your lecture!"

I don't know if I was more surprised or pleased. I immediately agreed to accompany Judy to her house, only a few miles from the hotel. She escorted me to the bedroom where I was given the choice of a number of fine suits, shirts and ties. *All* of which fit me as if custom tailored!

Imagine the discussion at her dinner table that night. "Hi honey, how was your day at the office? You won't believe what happened here this morning..."

## Chef Jeff

You know, there really *is* something *magical* about Disney's Magic Kingdom. Their customer service is *exemplary*. In a word, it's *extreme*.

My son, Brendon, and I had enjoyed an adventure-filled morning in the Kingdom. We were more than ready for a lunch break. We happened upon one of Disney's many dining facilities – The Crystal Palace.

Though it *looked* magical, reality set in rapidly when we saw the number of guests ahead of us. There was a long line outside, waiting just to enter names into the queue. An enormous deck was filled with those waiting to be seated.

We made our way up the stairs toward the hostess stand. Disney employees were decked out in dress of the Gatsby era. Half way up the stairs toward the stand, we were greeted by one of the hosts. He welcomed us, took our name and number in the party, and handed us a slip to give to the host at the top.

Moments later, we reached the top of the steps, to be greeted again by another host and hostess. The hostess took the slip and welcomed us to the Crystal Palace. She told us that our table would be ready in approximately 20 minutes. I explained that I was on a special low-carbohydrate diet, and asked if I could just sneak a peak at the buffet.

The hostess asked another employee, Judy, to show us to the buffet. Judy escorted us past the crowd on the deck, and into the Crystal Palace. The dining room was immense (seating perhaps a couple hundred or more). And, it was gorgeous. Judy told me that in the past, she had worked on the 'line' preparing the buffet. She assured me that the food was absolutely wonderful.

"Oh, I'm sure its great. I have no doubt. The reason I asked to *see* the buffet is that I'm on a low-carbohydrate diet. I just wanted to see if there's anything that I can eat."

"Well come on with me. Let's take a look. I'm sure there's plenty you can enjoy".

We walked the buffet. It was gorgeous. I asked Judy some specific questions about the preparation of each of the dishes. Was there any corn syrup, cornstarch, or sugar added? Were any of the meats marinated in any sauces that might have had these in them, as well? Unfortunately, my diet allows for such a very tiny amount of carbohydrate (30 to 40 grams daily) that even an unknown marinade could, metabolically, throw off an entire day.

Judy was great. She told me that the best way to be certain would be to ask the chef. I'd seen at *least* five chefs running in and out of the kitchen. Judy disappeared for a moment, returning with one of the chefs.

She returned with none other than the executive chef. "Hi, I'm Jeff. Welcome to Crystal Palace. I'm responsible for the entire menu. I'd be happy to answer any questions you have." I was *truly* impressed that Judy had been able to gain the attention of the man in charge – they were in the middle of serving the main meal of their day to several hundred guests.

"Hi Jeff, Tom Orent. Sorry to take you away from your work... perhaps you could answer a couple of quick questions."

"Certainly. It would be my pleasure."

I felt as if I was the only guest in the dining room. It hit me right between the eyes: *this*, is how it should work, *this* is extreme customer service. Surely Jeff could have sent any one of the chefs out to chat with me.

I explained the diet. Yes, there were many salads and side vegetable dishes that would readily fit my diet. *However*, the main dishes *all* had unacceptable high levels of carbohydrates.

"How 'bout if I prepare a piece of the flank steak that hasn't been marinated yet?"

"That would be terrific, thanks!"

"My pleasure. How would you like it done?"

"Medium well. And, would there be any chance of blackening it, Cajun style?" I don't know if I'd just gone off the deep end with expectations, or if perhaps subconsciously I was *testing* Chef Jeff. No matter. If he were willing to accommodate, I'd have a *great* lunch.

"Cajun it is. Do you like chicken?"

"Sure, why?"

"Why don't I roast up a chicken for you as well..." No, he didn't know I was writing a book, and *no,* there were no TV crews or microphones! This was simply an example of unbelievable customer service. I gratefully accepted the offer of the flank steak and chicken.

Chef Jeff escorted us back out to the deck, to wait our turn. He asked me to inform my server of our arrangement, and predicted that, by the time we were inside and ready for the buffet, my special low carbohydrate meal would be ready.

Or so he thought. Even with the best of intentions, sometimes things still screw up. Tom Peters would advise taking *advantage* of the screw up. Make a recovery impression far greater than you could have if things had gone smoothly.

Brendon and I returned out to the deck to wait our turn for seating. There were *masses* of people outside. Within five minutes Chef Jeff came up to me. "So sorry, sir. I lied. We don't have a single piece of the flank steak that hasn't already been marinated.

"Would you mind if I make you a Cajun prime rib? It's a far better cut, anyway."

The guy was beyond real.  He searched for me in an enormous crowd to ask if he could fix me a Cajun prime rib!  I couldn't disappoint him, so I agreed.

The prime rib was delicious, as was the chicken, and every side dish we tried.  The atmosphere was lovely – not easy when you're entertaining hundreds of families with small children.  The entire staff was attentive, warm and *truly* cared about the experience.

When the check came, Brendon guessed that there would be a significant charge beyond the fee for the usual buffet.

I certainly would have understood, and  been happy to pay whatever amount was requested.  However, in keeping with Chef Jeff's *Extreme* attitude, the check simply read, "One adult buffet, and one child."

## L'Espalier

Known for the finest dining Boston has to offer, L'Espalier is tucked away on a side street just off Boston's famed Newbury Street. If you didn't know it was there, you would never see or find it. Not a problem. *Everyone* familiar with fine dining knows the address.

From the moment the valet takes your car, to the last morsel of the dessert, L'Espalier *is* extreme customer service. The food is beyond description with mere words. One would need at least three of the five senses to *begin* to do justice to the fare.

This five-star establishment is tiny in size and grand in stature. Just walking in the door makes you feel very, extra special. But walking out, *that* was a new experience!

Our dinner reservation was for 10:00 p.m. (the mark of a successful spot, it was the *earliest* we could get). By the time we finished a leisurely multi-course experience, midnight had already passed.

As we began the short walk toward the exit, no less than ten uniformed (black tie, of course) wait staff assembled along our path. As if a military send-off, each of the ten thanked us and bid us a good evening! It wasn't until we'd passed the third or fourth one that it hit me – *this* was their final (well-rehearsed) *Wow* of the evening.

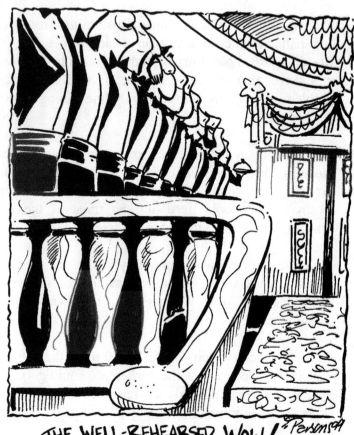

THE WELL-REHEARSED _WOW!_

## Maintaining *Sight* of Customer Service

It had been a long time since he'd last had his eyes checked. Will Reed scheduled a routine eye exam at his HMO, Harvard Pilgrim Health Care. His professional schedule made it difficult to find time for 'wellness' visits, but it was time.

The exam took place at Harvard Pilgrim's facility in Wellesley, Massachusetts. Mr. Reed was examined by a very caring and astute ophthalmologist who had recently completed her training at Yale.

"Mr. Reed, do you ever see *floaters*?"

"Well, yes, *frequently*."

"When was the last time you had your eyes *dilated*?"

"I can't remember. It's been a while."

"Do you have anyone who could drive for you after the visit, today?"

"Sure."

"Then I'd like to do that for you now, as part of today's exam."

The ophthalmologist proceeded to do the exam, including the dilation.

"I'd like to consult with my supervisor. I'll return in just a moment."

Together the two ophthalmologists examined and consulted. The senior doctor said, "Nice find, doctor."

They explained to Mr. Reed that he had two small holes in the retina of his left eye, in very close proximity to each other. The holes could connect, and if they did, there was a significant possibility he would lose sight in that eye.

"Mr. Reed, I've spoken to an eye surgeon in Kenmore Square. We'd like to have the problem corrected *immediately*. You are scheduled for laser surgery *this* afternoon!"

At the Kenmore Square facility, Mr. Reed was seated in a wheelchair and brought into a prep room for surgery. After the treatment, Mr. Reed was able to return home a few hours later.

With potential scheduling conflicts and the red tape to which we've all grown accustomed, a process which might have taken several days or weeks was accomplished in a span of hours. Mr. Reed is grateful for their expertise as *well* as their ability and commitment to making the *logistical* sequence painless.

## *Infiniti* **Customer Service!**

Whether a luxury or necessity, all cars become a major inconvenience when they need repair. It usually takes two, to get the car to and from the repair shop. A repair estimated to take a day takes a week – parts have to be ordered from East Oshkosh.

Infiniti of Natick, Massachusetts, changed my impression, for good. The first time I needed service on my Q45, I suffered all the usual pangs of anticipation. How long would I be without a car? How would I get back from the agency? How would I get around while they held it 'hostage?' What would it *cost*?

I'd purchased my "Q" used. It was a recovered stolen vehicle. The thieves had obliterated the VIN (vehicle identification number), but the State of New York had issued a new (arbitrary) number.

Did Infiniti treat me like a second-class citizen? Hardly. I sat with the service manager and explained the car's seedy history. He said that he'd do his best to trace its origin, to see if perhaps the original factory warranty was still intact. I didn't hold much hope for that one, though I thought it was nice that he suggested trying.

My sunroof motor needed replacement. It could run into considerable expense, but they'd call before anything was done.   There were three surprises to follow.

*Surprise Number One*: "Dr. Orent, here are the keys to a red Infiniti *I*30, waiting out back.  Enjoy the loaner. We'll give you a call once we've got more information for you."

*Surprise Number Two*: A couple days after I'd been driving my shiny new *I*30, I received a call from the service manager.  "Dr. Orent, we *were* able to trace the origin of your car.  A dealer sold it in upstate New York.  The warranty *is* still in effect, so the repair will be courtesy of Infiniti!"

I really couldn't believe they'd taken the time and trouble to trace the car – without the help of the original VIN.  And their efforts resulted in *Infiniti* taking responsibility for the costs of repair!

*Surprise Number Three*: When I returned to pick up my "Q," it had been cleaned.  *Inside* and out.  It looked better than ever, was in tip-top working condition, and didn't cost me a penny.  Infiniti removed the *stress* usually associated with car repair.

## *Sole* of the Organization

Customer Service doesn't need to be an exclusive right limited to those who live the lifestyles of the rich and famous. It should be a right for all.

Consider the Work Boot, an icon of the hardworking construction worker, logger, and laborer. Heavy upper, steel toes, and heavy, steel-shanked, rubber sole with deep grooves to provide traction... and, as a by-product, collect mud, which subsequently gets dumped on the kitchen floor upon return home.

A contractor has purchased his shoes from White Shoes, of Spokane, Washington, for years. He still has the same original upper shoes, first purchased more than 20 years ago! Cycling through several pairs, all the shoes have adopted the shape and manner of the wearer. When the soles wear out after many years of continuous use, he returns the shoes to Spokane for new soles.

One year, a new breed of construction boot appeared in the catalog, with a sole designed to provide grip without collecting clumps of mud. The contractor filled out the order form, the lady of the house waited with eager anticipation. The boots arrived and were immediately put into use.

Within the first year, however, the soles wore out. Uncommonly fast. So the boots went back with a note, "Please put regular style sole on, and bill my account."

Soon after, the boots were shipped back to the contractor -- with new soles, and a note:

"We have replaced the bottoms free of charge. The material we used in the boots was defective. We apologize for any inconvenience we may have caused."

---

*Extreme* Autopsy

This type of customer service is an *attitude*. It's adopted by the entire team and becomes a form of 'corporate culture.' It fosters *long*-term relationships, and *repeat* business.

## No Dogs *Allowed*

Three friends traveling in New Jersey arrived at their hotel late at night. It was early spring, still cold, damp, and raining. An aging Labrador Retriever, traveling with the three, was just as tired and looking forward to a good snooze in preparation for the next day.

They knew that hotels in the area often accepted dogs, but frequently required an additional fee. They were prepared to *smuggle* in their furry friend, if needed.

As they drove up to their destination, they saw a 20-story, single entrance hotel. The lobby was packed with a college swim team, noisily celebrating a championship win.

They checked in. The reservation was for one room with two queen size beds– but only one room with one king size bed was available. Like many guests, they were disappointed and angered that their requested room wasn't available. In the background, the athletes' loud voices and pounding feet set the stage for a sleepless night.

They asked if dogs were allowed, explaining that the dog was older, very clean, and really needed to sleep in a warm place. The young man at the desk looked disappointed as he said "No dogs."

Then he walked into the back office to speak with the night manager. She came to the desk and explained that the hotel manager was very strict about dogs. He'd allow rowdy college students, but no dogs. One of the travelers was prepared to sleep in the truck, to keep the dog warm.

The night manager smiled warmly at the three and said, "Drive around back and come in through the service entrance. Walk the dog up to the second floor, then you may take the elevator from there. The Manager has cameras in the lobby; don't bring her through here. Come through the back. Thank you for staying with us."

---

*Extreme* Autopsy

The night manager listened to the customers' needs, and set *policy* aside for the night. An *average* hotel made a *well above*-average impression on the travelers *and* their canine companion.

## *Sensitivity* to Sensitivity

Rochelle Johnson realized that she had a problem with one of her fillings. But unlike most people who could just call *any* dentist and get it taken care of with ease, Rochelle has a special concern. She has latex allergy, and knows to take it very seriously.

Patients *and* dental staff alike can suffer from latex allergy. The mildest reaction is contact dermatitis – a skin rash, limited to the area of contact. Symptoms could *also* be as dramatic as anaphylaxis – a systemic life-threatening allergic reaction.

The only dentist she'd known to take her condition seriously was more than four hours away, by car. Logistically it was just too difficult to drive eight hours round trip for a filling.

She reached out to a friend on the Internet, Colleen Sherman, who referred her to a dental clinic devoted to minimal use of latex. Rochelle found them *very* friendly, understanding of her needs, and up to date. They stock all the latest equipment.

Here is her account, word for word, as she described the *extremely* understanding attitude of her new dental "home." She e-mailed the following to her friend Colleen:

While I waited in the chair they showed me videos of a coral reef from a small screen TV. I then helped them take a picture of the offending tooth. When they used an anesthetic on me for the drilling and filling part of the procedure, there was *absolutely* no pain at all. The two men who worked on me were absolutely sweet and compassionate, and treated me like a queen (a far cry from my earlier experience this week with the dermatologist's receptionists). It is very affirming to work with professionals who treat you seriously and know just how ill you could get if they don't take good care of you. WE ARE NOT CRAZY, FOLKS."

Rochelle D. Johnson, MSW, LCSW-C

Her delight was predicated on this dental team's sensitivity to patients with latex allergy. The fact that she had such a negative experience with the dermatologist's staff is incredible! After all, wouldn't you imagine that team members in a dermatology office would be the *most* in tune with her problem!

## How the "Wild Ones" Got Their Name

Mother's account...

Last year my husband bought two sets of golf clubs from Sam's Club in Natick, Massachusetts. Wilson Sporting Goods manufactured the clubs, called "The Wild Ones." They were fine the first year, then....

This past month, our son, Tom, and *his* son, Brendon, came down to Cape Cod to visit us. They went to the driving range to hit golf balls.

Our son hit the ball an enormous distance with the driver. Astonishingly, the **head of the club flew off upon impact, and sailed almost as far as the ball had carried!**

Next, Tom tried the three wood, and the exact same thing occurred! The head of the club separated from the shaft, and again flew the distance. Fortunately, no one was injured. It could have been a disaster.

My husband tried to return the clubs to Sam's. The sales associate pointed out a sign on the wall – a manufacturer's defect return policy stating that damaged goods must be returned within 30 days.

A year *had* gone by, but we felt the circumstances warranted a second look.

"...THE CLUB HEADS *BARELY* TOUCHED THE TURF PRIOR TO LAUNCHING INTO THEIR ORBIT!"

I called the store again, and reached Maureen, a delightful claims associate. I told her that, in past years, my husband had done business directly with Sam Walton, and that Sam would have been appalled at the 30-day return policy. Defective was *defective*!

Maureen said, "Never mind Sam, *I'm* appalled. Please give me your name and telephone number and I will see that someone gets back to you directly." She promised to take my plight to the general manager.

Less than 15 minutes passed when a young man returned my call. He introduced himself as the new assistant operations manager, apologized, and took personal responsibility for the situation.

He said he had researched the history of the clubs; there were *numerous* complaints and they had accepted returns of all of the original clubs from the dissatisfied customers.

He invited me to bring the clubs back to him for a credit, not only for the damaged clubs, but also for the *entire* set. I accepted his offer, expressed my appreciation, and asked to speak to Maureen.

I thanked her for going that 'extra mile' in customer satisfaction. It was her *extreme* concern and personal attention, that revitalized our positive memory of Sam Walton."

My mother, Daisy Orent, related this story. I *swear* the club heads *barely* touched the turf prior to launching into their orbit!

## Flat, *not* "Soft"

Do you own a restaurant? A shoe store? A dry cleaners? Are you running a multi-national corporation? It makes little difference when it comes to the 'small stuff' that *irks* all of us at a 'gut' level. Whether it's potentially losing a repeat customer to the corner restaurant, or the devastating loss of a major foreign account, the 'small stuff' matters. It could make or break you.

Dr. Richard Carlson wrote a fabulous book entitled, Don't Sweat the Small Stuff -- and it's *all* Small Stuff. Great title and a great message, when it comes to learning not to take ourselves so seriously (Dr. Carlson's book became mandatory reading for my entire team). *BUT*, for those interested in the health and future fitness of their business, you *must* sweat the small stuff. And yes, it *is* ALL small stuff!

Could the fizz in a soft drink make *that* much difference? Well, maybe not the fizz alone... but watch what became of the fizz in this particular story:

Last spring, my family and I visited a restaurant on Cape Cod, Massachusetts. My soft drink was flat. I asked the waitress if there was something that could be done to replace it with a drink with some pep.

"Oh, that's because of the glasses. When the glasses are warm, the soft drinks lose all their fizz. At least that's what they *told* us."

I asked if she could try bringing another one, from a different part of the restaurant. She left for the kitchen again. From my limited experience, tending bar in college, this shouldn't be rocket science: the $CO_2$ canister mixes with the syrup, and voila! A soft drink with little teeny bubbles. If the mixture is wrong, or the $CO_2$ empty, the drink is flat.

The waitress returned with another. Just as flat. It had the appearance of ice tea. I asked her if the bartender would mind changing the $CO_2$ canister.

"It wouldn't make any difference. I was here when the vendor told us that this is the best they can do with our glasses. In fact, *all* of our soft drinks are like that!"

She was right. My son Brendon had a root beer. He tasted it. How right she was! Not a fizz or bubble in sight! Moments later she returned with two bottled soft drinks, a Cola for me, a root beer for Brendon "We had these *last* summer... I don't know if it will be any better, considering how long it's been here."

Turns out she was right, they were as bad as the bar-dispensed versions. Although we told her what we thought of the bottled ones, she *not* only charged me for mine, but also added an *extra* charge for Brendon's! The menu indicated that the kids' meals included a free soft drink. When I queried why the *additional* charge (for a soda he wouldn't drink), she replied, "The kids' meals only include soda from the bar. **We *have* to charge if a bottle is served!**"

Neither father nor son had anything to drink with the meal, yet we were charged for both drinks (instead of the one we anticipated).

*Extreme* Autopsy

It's really sad just how easily *most* customer service issues can be solved. In fact, a *bad* situation cannot only be "solved," but made into a terrific opportunity --if the team's attitude is focused on service.

How? In this case, the waitress could have run next door to the pharmacy to purchase two fresh bottles of soft drinks (assuming this was a one-time problem... or she'd go crazy *and* broke). What a simple solution to win over the hearts of her customers!

If she had come back to the table and told us that she ran next door for the drinks, we'd have been duly impressed. Equally important, we'd have enjoyed our meals! And *returned!*

A longer term solution would be either to find a new vendor who can figure out how to make the soft-drink machine work properly, *or*, simply switch to bottled soft-drinks... Just don't serve bottles that sat outside in the heat all last year!

## Sweat the *Small* Stuff

Good "old-fashioned customer service." 1964. The Beverly Hills Hotel, Beverly Hills, California. Where the Hollywood stars can be seen. The hotel had developed an international reputation for excellence – by sweating the *small* stuff.

Dr. Stewart Rosenberg, and his wife, Nancy, checked in. They had a quaint little cottage with a kitchenette. The Rosenbergs were traveling with friends, one of whom was an insulin-dependent diabetic. Their friends didn't have a kitchenette, and needed the insulin refrigerated. They left it in the Rosenbergs' kitchenette.

Mrs. Rosenberg is allergic to the perfumes in many soaps, so she brought along a bar of Ivory Soap. After using the Ivory in the shower, she left the open bar in the dish on the side of the tub.

Before heading to Disneyland, they stopped at the front desk to discuss their cottage. It was far away from the main hotel building, and overlooked rubbish disposal in the parking lot. The registration folks told them that they'd keep their eyes out for a new room; if anything became available, they'd be able to move.

After the day at Disneyland, they returned to learn that the hotel management had taken the liberty of moving their belongings into the new room. When they'd left the original room for the day, clothes were strewn all over, the hypoallergenic soap was in the tub and insulin in the fridge...

In the new room, their clothes were all neatly folded and tucked away and the Ivory soap was in the shower. But, what about their friend's tiny, life-saving vial of insulin?

They found a bouquet of red roses on the dresser, with an attached note written by the staff member who had moved their things. He said that he hoped they would find this room more to their liking, and left his name in case there were any questions after the move. He added that, since the main hotel rooms didn't have a kitchenette, he "took the liberty of moving a portable refrigerator into your room, for Dr. Rosenberg's insulin."

---

*Extreme* Autopsy

Often, *extreme* doesn't require *monumental* overwhelming effort, high expense, or lavish gifts. Extreme service may be realized by *extreme* attention to the little details.

---

## VIP *One*-Star Customer Service!

How better to teach the finer points of VIP 5-Star Customer Service than let the team experience it for themselves?  I decided we should take a trip, by chauffeured limousine, into Boston's Ritz Carlton.

We'd conference during the ride, in style.  Everyone would enjoy being pampered by the limousine ride and the Ritz staff during our annual meeting.  Or so we thought.

We were happy to have such a comfortable ride, as it was 102 degrees that summer day.  When the limo arrived, I noticed that the roof vinyl was a bit road-worn; but the driver was nice enough, and we were all anticipating an enjoyable and productive day.

Our dress was appropriate for our destination -- the Ritz -- and we were happy to duck inside the climate-controlled limo and beat the heat.  It didn't seem all that cool inside, but I figured it would take a few minutes and then we'd be fine.

In fact, it never got any better.  The driver apologized to me, saying that he was having difficulty with the air-conditioning!  It was 103F outside, and about 98F inside, and rising!

We were extremely uncomfortable, and asked if they could bring a different limo for the return ride at the end of the day.  He was very accommodating, extremely apologetic, and immediately agreed to the request. The mid-afternoon sun was predicted to bring temperatures upwards of 105F. We were delighted he could oblige. Or so we thought!

The meeting at the Ritz was terrific. It is a highly recommended exercise for leaders interested in developing their teams' grasp of *extreme* customer service.

As we got into the return limo, a wave of unbearable heat overcame us. It was almost unbreathable. We were toasts! The "new" limo had *NO* air-conditioning! There was little we could do about it, as everyone had their own plans for the evening, and looking for a new service would take more time than we could afford. Or so we thought!

We were roughly *half*way home when a loud noise from beneath haunted us. Our limo was dying! In short order, we had *no* ride. We were stuck on the side of the Massachusetts Turnpike, dressed to the nines, in 105 degrees Fahrenheit weather, with no place to hide from the sun.

Our formally dressed team, standing outside the limo, turned more than a few heads. In fact, so many heads turned that a car went right into the center guardrail! The driver wasn't hurt -- but the cars to follow piled right into him, as their divers stared at *us* on the side.

It was like a poorly written "B" movie. Moments later, the driver of a pick-up truck, staring at my team, failed to see the stalled traffic ahead. Too late to stop, he swerved off the road, and came within three feet of killing my entire team!

"..NO PLACE TO HIDE FROM THE SUN,... OUR
FORMALLY DRESSED TEAM OUTSIDE THE LIMO
TURNED MORE THAN A FEW HEADS."

It took the Limousine Company 90 minutes to get us a replacement ride! Although our *third* limo did have air-conditioning, it mattered very little: after all, by the time our third car arrived, it was almost winter!

---

**Extreme Autopsy**

There's no excuse for the way this company operated their business. I would have expected an ordinary taxi to have air-conditioning, and wheels that would last until our destination. The owner of the Company should be ashamed to run a VIP service that doesn't measure up even to a *One*-Star standard. The very least that should have been done was to *immediately* call cabs or some other form of transportation for us, which could have rescued us from a very dangerous spot on I-90... somewhere west of Boston.

## Four Seasons.

## *Five Stars.*

What is it about the Four Seasons Hotel and their Aujourd'Hui restaurant?  Why, after one visit, is the most seasoned service connoisseur hooked?  There is no one answer.  Perhaps it's their *team* approach to service.  Or maybe it's their ability to see the four letters emblazoned upon all of our foreheads: MMFI (see *Mary and Ali*).

From the moment you arrive, until the Four Seasons fades in the rear-view mirror, **you feel important**.

One person is no more important than any other.  In fact, even if you could make a case to counter that statement, it wouldn't matter.  You are *only* as important as you *feel*.  Much of our individual successes in life, and our abilities to achieve our personal bests, are intertwined with our self-images.

It makes up for an enormous amount of the 'small stuff,' when you 'make me feel important.'  Hailey said, "Chances are, if I feel better about myself when I'm with you, I'm going to want to spend *more* time with you!"

How often have you made reservations, at some fancy restaurant, **only to find out that your reserved time only got you as far as the bar?** "Yes, Madame.  I see your reservation right here.  If you would be so kind as to follow me, we will be happy to seat you for a drink until your table is ready."

Recently I dined at just such a spot in Las Vegas. After getting tired of my Diet Cokes and lime (my most potent drink), we decided to mosey back over to the hostess stand – to make it known that we weren't their best bar customers. Coincidentally, within 60 seconds, we were seated for dinner.

Within two minutes of our arrival at Aujourd'Hui, we were escorted to our table. As you walk through the dining area, you can't help but notice the distance between tables; it's extraordinarily far. They easily could have placed 30 percent more tables; instead, they chose to foster a sense of 'private dining' in the middle of a very busy restaurant. We could neither hear nor see much of what was happening at any of the neighboring tables.

Within just moments of seating, we were presented with four different kinds of bread... and *three* wait staff! One could have simply chosen to dine on the bread, and called it a meal!

When it was time to deliver meals to a table, two or three wait staff would team together in a seemingly effortless *orchestral* maneuver. In fact, I watched, on more than one occasion, a group huddle; not unlike a football team before the big play, the wait staff would meet in the center of the room -- three or four of them -- and literally *huddle* in a small circle. One would coordinate their next play, and they'd break into different directions of action.

You can't feel important with crumbs all over your place so, between all the courses, they'd come over and tidy up any crumbs we'd scattered about. They performed each task with efficiency, and with a smile. They were unimposing; *we* were their guests.

The food is always delicious, and I've never left feeling hungry. But exactly *what* did we buy? Fifteen percent of our check reflected their delectable cuisine; the other 85% were the 'sizzle.' One could easily find similar food at a number of eateries in town. But **when you feel as wonderful about the *experience* as you do about the product, you'll remember, you'll return, and refer.**

## *Pre*-managing Expectations

Back in **The *Extreme* Dream, Part III: Technical Support**, we touched upon the concept of 'under-promise, over-deliver.' This is known as *pre*-managing expectations. If you become successful at the art of under-promise and over-deliver, you may realize successes beyond your wildest dreams.

Let's look at some examples. Mrs. Johnson brings her car to the shop for service. She describes a noise in the front end, as well as the need for routine 30,000-mile maintenance. Jerry, the service manager, determines how long he thinks it will take to do the job.

Mrs. Johnson explains that she'd really like to have her car back by Friday, at noon, if possible. She and Mr. Johnson are going up north for the weekend, and *his* car is too old to make the trip comfortably. Jerry knows he can get the routine maintenance part done, but isn't certain about resolving the noise problem. After all, until the shop diagnoses it, they won't really know what they're in for.

But he doesn't want to disappoint dear Mrs. Johnson, either, so he 'promises' that she'll have her car by Friday afternoon. Of course, Murphy's Law of over-promising kicks into overdrive. When Mrs. Johnson calls on Friday morning around 11:00, the receptionist tells her that her car is "all set." Delighted that things have worked out as anticipated, Mrs. Johnson gets a ride over to the shop from a neighbor.

Mrs. J. pays the bill (which seems awfully reasonable) and heads home to pack for the weekend trip. After meeting her husband and preparing their things, they head out onto the road.

Just after dusk, they hear the front-end noise again. Within moments, there's a loud thud, and the elderly couple is stranded on the side of the dark unfamiliar highway, wondering what to do next.

Jerry *knew* that Mrs. Johnson needed the car back before noon on Friday. His crew completed the routine service, but didn't hear the noise that Mrs. Johnson had described. Had they had more time, they might have found the intermittent problem that inevitably led to their frightening breakdown in the middle of nowhere, that night.

---

### *Extreme* Autopsy

What *should* Jerry have done? If he had thought there was *any* chance her car would not have been ready, he should have told her when she dropped it off. At *least* tell her that there's a chance they may not solve the mystery noise on short-notice, although the routine work would be no problem.

Armed with the truth, and a fair expectation of their ability to solve her problems, Mrs. Johnson would have had a better opportunity to make a safer decision about her weekend travel plans.

---

Dr. Howard Farran is one of the first dentists in the United States to teach this type of business theory to dentists (I've since *stolen* it for *my* seminars). Dr.

Farran discusses the case of Mr. Moore, who underwent a routine tooth-colored filling.

"Doc, is this thing going to hurt when the anesthetic wears off?"

"Naw, it shouldn't. It *really* wasn't that deep."

What do *you* think will happen? Of course. Murphy's Law says that if you tell a dental patient that there shouldn't be any discomfort afterwards, then, of course, there will be! *And* you're in hot water... since *that* tells signals bells to go off in the patient's mind – something *must* have gone wrong.

When you take a dental drill, turning at approximately 300,000 revolutions per minute, and remove a section of live tooth – *even* if it *isn't* that deep – there's *always* the possibility of some post-operative discomfort or sensitivity.

---

*Extreme* Autopsy

*If* you tell a patient that there *is* possibly going to be some discomfort for a period after, then you win *either* way. If it is a bit sensitive for a day or two, then you were *right.* If it never bothers her at *all* then you were a hero. But *why* on Earth would you want to play Russian roulette with Murphy's Law?

---

Of course this need not be a dental patient. Pause for moment and see if you can relate a similar scenario from your *own* field of interest. Let's say you're delivering a brand-new car.

"Mrs. McCarthy, we hope you enjoy your brand-new coupe for many years to come. Remember, I want to be the *first* to know if *any* little thing needs adjustment – after all, you didn't just buy the car, you've got *me* with it! I'll have the service folks doing tap dances to get you in the *very next day.*"

Of course, you'll want to make sure that you have the authority and the ability to get her in for any 'tweaking' the day after she calls. *And* you've got to make yourself available when she calls!

Mrs. McCarthy drives her brand-new coupe home, and she adores it. There is a switch on the dash that doesn't seem to be working, and the brakes feel a bit sticky... but she knows that *you* told her to expect a minor adjustment here or there. After all, she also knows that you'll pick up her call, *and* 'sneak' her into the service department the very next day.

What about the opposite scenario: the salesperson doesn't mention *anything* at all about the possibility of minor immediate needs. Instead, he reminds her to come in for a 30,000-mile routine quick check. Mrs. McCarthy very well may be embarrassed to call about little things, especially so early. Instead, when she drives her bridge club friends, they ask her about these little nuisance items... instead of *complimenting* her on her lovely new car.

I once performed a dental whitening procedure for a new patient, Mrs. Glick. My staff and I were usually *very* careful to let our patients know what to expect, how much whiter their teeth will become.

Regarding whitening: when we do our job correctly, we use a shade guide (a set of simulated teeth with a wide spectrum of known tooth colors) during the consultation. Once we've chosen the color we think most-closely approximates the patient's existing natural teeth, we'll record the shade into their record, *and* hold the selected shade tab next to *his/her* teeth – showing our finding while the patient holds a mirror.

The patient has the opportunity to agree or disagree that our selection does in fact match *his/her* teeth. Once agreed, **it's *our* job to provide a *realistic* set of expectations**. This very step is the Number One most critical factor in our ability to under-promise and *over*-deliver.

We blew it. In retrospect, as far as we can tell, no one on the staff told Mrs. Glick what to expect. We know for a fact that most whitening patients will improve *at least* two shades on the particular scale that we use. Some will do far better.

Mrs. Glick's teeth *were* shade C-3, a *very* dark and unsightly color. We should have shown her the C-3 tab. "Mrs. Glick, here's the C-3 shade tab. You'll note that it very closely approximates *your* natural tooth color."

We'd then take the C-2 shade-matching tab (a slightly brighter shade in the same basic grayish color range) hold it up next to her teeth, hand her a mirror, and say, "Mrs. Glick, this is *C-2*. **You'll be guaranteed to reach at *least* a C-2, with home whitening**. Some patients do better than that; however, if you don't do at *least* that well, we'll refund the entire whitening fee."

Apparently this conversation never took place. Mrs. Glick's newly whitened teeth were gorgeous. She was a rare exception to the one or two shade rule. Her teeth had not only lightened several shades; they had also jumped from one color group to another. Initially her teeth were one of the darkest of the C range, or grays. Upon reexamination, she had achieved a jump into the B range (the best colors on this particular scale). She was now a B-1.

So that you might appreciate a B-1... *most* of the models on the covers of *Vogue* and *Glamour* are in the neighborhood of B-1. It is *rare* that a patient could achieve that dramatic a result with a simple whitening treatment.   Whitening *is* very effective, but to a achieve a jump from C-3 to B-1 typically requires the placement of laminate porcelain veneers (an ultra-thin layer of sculpted porcelain that allows us to modify shade, shape, texture, size, almost at will).

I entered the treatment room for the follow-up appointment, unaware that we had neglected to let her know what to expect with home whitening. "Hello, Mrs. Glick, how are you today? How'd you do with your whitening treatment?"

"I'm fine, thank you, doctor... but the whitening didn't really work."

"Really (it's *rare* that whitening simply doesn't 'work'). May I take a look?"

I grabbed a shade guide and compared her new shade with the old. Sure enough, she'd achieved B-1. Unbelievable. What an *incredible* result (I thought to *myself*). "Mrs. Glick, it looks like you've done *really* well! You started with C-3 and jumped to a B-1. Your result is far more than we'd ever anticipate (doctor, open mouth, insert foot)."

"Really, doctor? I don't see much of a change at all. If I'd realized that *this* was all I could expect, I would never have had it done in the first place. I wanted *really* white!"

The above incident occurred at my office in September of 1998. Although "Mrs. Glick" isn't the patient's real name, every other detail is real. We ended up giving back the entire fee, and likely losing a patient for good. it was a very unfortunate outcome, given that her results were clinically outstanding!

What would have happened if I had done my job properly, and showed her the anticipated results? What would she have said if I'd held up a C-2 shade tab and told her to expect at *least* a C-2 with home whitening? The answer is obvious. She would have looked at me as if I had two heads, and she most certainly would have declined the treatment. If "Mrs. Glick" couldn't see much of a change from C-3 to B-1, then she would *never* have opted for the treatment if given the appropriate information prior to commencing.

## Fine, Is Not

Fine really *isn't*.  What?  That's right.  When someone
tells you that everything was 'fine,' they're likely
telling you there are problems.

You've gone out dining at a local restaurant you've
been to before, on occasion.  It's a nice place, though it
wouldn't appear in *Gourmet* magazine.  Your waiter
was polite and efficient.  No complaints.  The rolls
were a little tough, but certainly nothing to make a fuss
over (you've been dying to start that popular new low-
carbohydrate diet, anyway, and this was an ideal start).

Your meal was nice, though your wife's steak was a
little undercooked.  They took care of that in a jiffy,
and were very apologetic.  Overall, the service and the
food were fine, and you enjoyed yourselves.

At the next table, Mr. and Mrs. Bob Harding enjoyed
*their* evening, as well: she had the salmon, he had the
lobster.    Though they had a reservation, it seems
several earlier parties lingered, so the Hardings were
seated a bit late.  They, too, thought their waiter was
acceptable.   Neither actually complained about the
food, but Mrs. Harding told Mr. that the salmon was on
the tough side.  They'd been here before, and someday
they'd be back, again…maybe.

On the way out that evening, when the Maitre D' asked
if they'd enjoyed their dinners, both couples responded

identically.  *Both* said that everything was *"Fine."*
What's wrong with *fine?*  Everything! 'Fine' is an
indication that problems exist that weren't significant
enough to warrant 'bothering' the management. .
'Fine' should scare the hell out of you.

Neither couple wanted to make an issue out of the
'little' things that weren't quite right.  But, add *those*
little things with the few experienced by the couple
near the drafty fireplace, plus the others who waited
too long.  How about the party of eight who were split
into two fours (tired of waiting for a 'reserved' table
that never materialized)… you begin to get the picture.

Last week, I stayed at a hotel in Pennsylvania while on
a business trip.  It was a fairly upscale hotel.  There
were a few minor things about my stay that *easily*
could have been improved – but likely never will be
addressed.

I had no time for, or interest in, complaining about the
little annoyances:  heat that wouldn't regulate evenly
(very hot or too cold).  Or a television that looked like
one of the first color sets ever made; and not a single,
accessible  plug for my laptop (I often find it necessary
to move the bed to find a plug!).   Truly, these
annoyances are **nothing worth taking *my* time to
mention – but in the long run, these things do add
up**, and *may* help   influence a decision to return in the
future.

How do I know that 'Fine' could mean problems?
Easy: at checkout, the clerk *mechanically* asked how
everything was.  I *mechanically* answered, "Fine."

I did complain *one* time in Florida, when there were no working elevators. On Day One of my stay, one of the two elevators had an 'Out of Service' sign posted. The *other* one stopped at *each* floor, of its own free will!  I asked the clerk at the desk if he was aware that the 'working' elevator seemed to be malfunctioning.  He told me that he was *not* aware of any problems, and that the other elevator was closed for renovations and upgrading.

By the third day of my stay, neither elevator worked. Six flights of stairs, two or three times a day, for the next couple days.  *That* was beyond my 'fine' tolerance! The entire stay was free, but I'd still never go back.

Did you ever buy groceries -- only to get home before noticing that all was not just right?  A couple of the eggs were cracked.  Maybe the grapes were *really* sour (that's why you're supposed to eat some at the store, first!).  Or the scanner made an error.  One of the national TV newsmagazines did a piece on scanner accuracy: the percentage of errors was *appalling*.

How many of us would take the time to either *call* the grocery store, or return one item?  I applaud those who do, but fear that they are in the minority.

Have you noticed that big supermarket chains   are creating smaller 'boutique-like' grocery stores? They've become very popular of late; the service is outstanding, mistakes are less common, and their *attitude* is one of *extreme* customer service.  Wild Harvest is one such New England example. Owned by Star Market, they've created an almost cult-like following. The last few times I visited the Framingham store, I heard more than one person comment, "It's *fun* to shop here." **In *all* my years of shopping at the major markets, I've *never* heard anyone express a sentiment like that.**

At Wild Harvest, you *know* that if you have a question or concern, no matter *who* you approach for help, you'll be happy you asked. You truly feel like their 'guest.' Instead of pointing to the far corner of the store, they'll *walk* you there personally. At the checkout, they *always* smile, and greet you as if you were the most important person in their day.

# Conclusion

I.) Focus, and Venn Diagrams

How is it possible to have the laser-like focus of *extreme*ly great service organizations, while still meeting the broad range of needs of *all* people? It *isn't*. In <u>Raving Fans</u>, Ken Blanchard pinpoints basic prerequisite principles he feels set the stage for *extreme* customer service.

First, Blanchard suggests you define your vision; just what is it that you want to offer? FedEx did a world-class job of creating a concise vision: "Absolutely, positively overnight, *guaranteed.*" They didn't do that by trying to deliver *every* possible type of package and service. Rather, they limited their focus to their laser-like vision.

Second, Blanchard recommends finding out what your *customer* wants! Neat idea, eh? But think about it. How many times have we come up with (what we thought were) absolutely dynamite ideas, only to find the market didn't want them?

Figure out where the overlap exists between *your* vision, and what *they* (your customers) *want*. Remember Venn Diagrams? Your success lies within the *overlap* between your market's desires and your own.

How do you meet the needs that fall outside the overlap? You *don't* (necessarily). Become famous for exceeding your customers' expectations within the above-defined realm (the overlap).

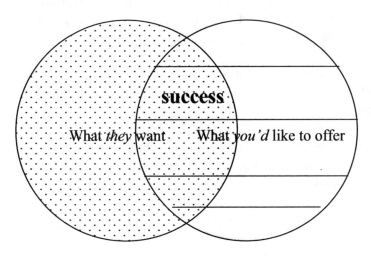

II.) "We're not *in* Customer Service"

If you believe that you are not 'in' *customer service,* then you're right, you're not. But don't feel that you might not benefit *immensely* by *getting* into it! We are *all* in customer service, like it or not.

It doesn't matter *who* you serve... or *where* you are in the food chain. You must determine *exactly who* your customer is! If your job doesn't put you directly in front of the public, figure out who **benefits from what you do**. There's your customer. (Of course you may be hard pressed to apply this if stranded alone on a deserted island. Otherwise, *figure* it out!)

III.) Measure to Improve

You've acknowledged the need for *extreme* customer service, and found your niche within the overlap. What you desire to deliver coincides with a need in the real world.

Great. Now figure out how you've been doing so far. Why? Lots of reasons. **Measure it and it will improve** is a solid business axiom. The act of measurement alone will usually result in significant improvement. But that's only the beginning. If you measure correctly, you may uncover **disaster waiting to happen**.

Take care to choose methodology *wisely*. It's far *easier* to rely on written feedback satisfaction surveys than to elicit feedback by calling customers one at a time. Don't be lulled into complacency. Harry Beckwith, in his best seller *Selling the Invisible*, warns of the fallacies involved in trusting written feedback:

*"For a dozen reasons, conduct ORAL SURVEYS, not written ones...* phone surveys usually produce more revealing results... a **person's voice conveys feelings that written words often obscure**...Oral surveys more accurately show *exactly* what the person being interviewed thinks and feels. An oral survey says you value their opinion."

First of all, most people don't take the written survey nearly as seriously as they do a human being on the phone asking the questions. Second, according to Beckwith, the **written survey can miss the *tone* of the respondent – and thus the message.**

An example of the power of the *spoken* word, versus written, follows: One of the services offered by Gems Publishing, USA is called Gems POLL (**Public Opinion Learning Lab** - 1-888-880-GEMS). We phone a sample of patients recently seen by our clients.

We have an incredibly high request to response ratio. Once you reach someone by phone and explain, for example, that you're calling on behalf of their doctor or dentist to help improve their service, people cooperate. Conversely, the number of people who respond to a written survey is considerably lower: in fact, respondents usually are only the ones who rave praise, or *hate* you. Though both are necessary, you're missing the bulk of your reason for being.

A dentist in northern California contracted our services for a P.O.L.L. Russell Dusablon, one of our highly skilled surveyors, made the calls. Russell elicited a *number* of 'gems' from the doctor's patients: thoughts **not likely to have been expressed otherwise**.

For instance, a woman (we'll call her Mrs. Jones) told Russell that she'd be happy to participate, and to just give all 'Strongly Agrees,' since she absolutely *adored* the doctor. Russell knew better. He asked Mrs. Jones to humor him, and asked a set of 30 questions, one at a time.

All answers were 'Strongly Agrees' until he got to a question about the hygienist. When Russell asked if she felt that the hygienist was caring and gentle, Mrs. Jones didn't answer as quickly as she had previously. Russell, sensing her hesitation, said, "Mrs. Jones, please be *brutally* honest with me."

Mrs. Jones said, "Well, the doctor has two hygienists. Sarah is a sweetheart. But the other one, I forget her name – well, she is very rough." Mrs. Jones told Russell that she'd never told the doctor.

Mrs. Jones is more like your mainstream customer than you'd ever realize. When they have a problem, they'd rather *not* tell you about it. In many instances, they'll leave you for another before facing the stress of confrontation.

When Russell finished his questions, he asked Mrs. Jones if there were *anything* at all she'd like to add, something that she wanted to tell the doctor, but never had. There sure was. Mrs. 'Extremely Satisfied' Jones wasn't...when it came to the doctor's payment policy: he requires full payment for services at their start. Mrs. Jones told Russell that it seemed unfair; she didn't mind making a substantial payment at the start, but preferred to pay the remainder upon completion of the treatment.

What did this doctor find out about one of his most 'satisfied' patients? She was, perhaps, one or two additional complaints away from leaving the practice!

Maybe the next time they ask to collect that full payment up front, will be the time she sits in the waiting room for 45 minutes. Or the next time the B-team 'hygienist from hell' rips at her mouth, and tells her that if only she would care more about her personal hygiene, maybe the cleanings wouldn't hurt so much!

Farfetched? Hardly. Another 'Extremely Satisfied' patient of this same doctor told Russell that everything about this doctor was incredible. Again, the expectation was for 100% "Strongly Agrees.' If this had been a *written* survey, that may have been the result. And it *would* have been *wrong*.

Everything was going great until the question about comforts in the waiting room. "Mrs. Smith, please respond to the following question with Strongly Agree, Agree, Disagree, or Strongly Disagree: The waiting room is very comfortable and inviting."

"Well, it's just a typical waiting room."

"Does that mean that you don't agree with the statement?"

"Well, no. It's not *bad*, it's just that it's a doctor's waiting room!"

"So would you say that you Disagree, or Strongly Disagree?"

"Strongly Disagree."

Mrs. Smith later told us that her doctor was incredible: she had never met anyone more caring, with genuine interest and concern for their patients. Her responses to the entire survey were "Strongly Agree"... *except,* that, well, "it's just a typical doctor's waiting room!"

What's the significance of her response? First, it points out that a customer or patient who is overwhelmingly positive about your business may still have issues about which you should know – but which will likely *never* surface until it's too late.

Second, examine for a moment the specific question, and her answer. What Mrs. Smith said, in essence, is that the doctor's waiting room *met* her expectations. She didn't *expect* anything more than some basic chairs and old magazines, in "a doctor's waiting room."

Why then, if the doctor *met* her expectations, should we be at all concerned? Because 'meeting' expectations will only lull you into a false sense of security. *Extreme* customer service is *based* upon exceeding expectations at *every* conceivable opportunity.

What could one do to *exceed* expectations in a 'waiting room?' At the Center for Esthetic Dentistry, my reception desk had a brass and marble plaque that reads "concierge." The health history (a new patient's very first impression) suggests that one might ask the concierge, if interested, for a glass of white wine while completing the form. A beautiful, freestanding salt-water fish tank is the centerpiece around which the seating is designed. Exotic tropical fish entertain folks from all angles of view.

'Wellness' is on peoples' minds, today. Our reception area has an extensive display of health and wellness information from *other* practitioners and specialists in our community. *Their* patient education information is available to those with interest or concerns.

The wonderful aroma of fresh bread fills the atmosphere, as our staff bakes bread twice daily for our patients – our *friends*. Smooth jazz plays softly in the background, while a Sony Playstation awaits the little ones in a private cubby off to the side. Of course, the video game's sound has been deactivated and channeled through headphones to maintain the atmosphere we've created.

What about simple thoughtfulness for the comforts and necessities? Just off our reception area (a ten-foot walk, to afford privacy) is the restroom (see the chapter "The Spa" to review the *extreme* comforts available to guests visiting our facilities).

But there is one thing in our restroom that many consider **an essential need, – yet we know is addressed by less than 1% of dentists** throughout the United States and Canada: a selection of feminine hygiene products. What a simple, basic need, easily addressed. Yet we, as a profession, have consistently overlooked them for our 'guests.' In the Center for Esthetic Dentistry's restroom is a closet discretely marked with "♀."

Initially, one might suspect that the lack of thought regarding this particular need stems from a male dominated profession, but perhaps we can attribute it to a lack of awareness. Dentistry is a changing profession with respect to the gender mix. Currently, the entering classes in dental schools are 50:50 male to female.

I recently asked my audience (more than 500 dentists and team members) how many of their offices had addressed this basic female need. It was with *shock* that we all realized how insensitive we'd really been: only three people raised their hands.

Back to oral surveys. In addition to missing vocal *tones,* written surveys often miss the crucial respondents *altogether.* Consider this quote from Dr. Ken Blanchard's <u>Raving Fans</u>.

---

"I ate the cold dinner.  I was hungry."

"Did you complain?"

"No, I didn't.  I was so fed up, I didn't even fill out the customer service card that was on the table... *waste of time and a waste of ink.* I bet that restaurant wouldn't even read the card, much less *do* anything about it."

---

It truly doesn't take much more than thoughtfulness and imagination to *exceed* the expectations of guests in *your* business. Adopt a 'guest mentality.' You, and your team, should **treat each and every customer/patient/client as if he/she were a guest in your home.**

How would you meet and greet a guest in your home? What would you say first?  Would you offer something to drink? To eat? Would you show the guest around? Or would you allow your guest to wander in alone, to unfamiliar unfriendly territory?

Simply treating each and every person as if he or she was a guest in your home will go a *long* way toward exceeding expectations. Remember, "in the land of the blind, the one-eyed man is king!"

The unspoken word can be deadly. If you've not had a survey done for *your* client base recently, it's *beyond* time. There are many excellent national firms waiting to meet your research needs.

**(Gems Public Opinion Learning Lab** may be reached, *toll-free* at 1-888-880-GEMS).

Expectations are rising. The average level of customer service if falling. Crossing that chasm is a *major* step toward getting to 'YES.'

Your future survival and prosperity is deeply rooted in your ability to create "Raving Fans'" (Dr. Ken Blanchard), your "Pursuit of *Wow*" (Dr. Tom Peters)... your *willingness* to deliver "Extreme Customer Service."

## Author's note:

*Every* story in this book is true. After a brief (pardon the pun) discussion with my attorney, all names and locations in the *extreme*ly *bad* customer service stories were changed – to protect the guilty.

## Invitation:

If *you* have an extreme (good *or* bad) customer service story you'd like to share, please send it, with permission reprint, to Dr. Tom Orent:

C/o Gems Publishing, USA
12 Walnut Street
Framingham, MA 01702

Fax: 508-861-1550
E-mail: Tom@1000gems.com

As You Can See,
There's a Million Dollar Bill
at the Top of This Page
and There's More
Where That Came From Because...

# I'll Show You How to Discover the HIDDEN WEALTH in Your Dental Practice Absolutely FREE – if You ACT NOW!

Dear Friend,

No matter how hard you work you just can't seem to get ahead -- or give your family the things dentists' families enjoyed when you were a kid.

You know why -- managed care, patients who refuse needed treatment, staff hassles -- all the things that leave you driving to work every day with stress as your passenger. Which is why it's so important that you read this letter, and learn how you can:

**Totally Obliterate the Things That Are Killing Your Practice and Double...Even Triple Your Income**

You know me. I'm Dr. Tom Orent. You've read my columns, maybe even bought my books or attended my seminars.

People call me "the Gems Guy" because my easy-to-implement practice and income-building ideas (GEMS!) have changed the lives of 16,543 dentists for the better.

"My life feels forever changed as we have been averaging almost an extra **$50,000** in production, above and beyond what was once 'normal'". -- Dr. Kory Wegner, Milwaukee, WI

My gems were born out of necessity. My practice had one foot in the grave and needed strategies that were quick and effective (not to mention cheap). And I discovered a ton of them, with the result that in just three years I went from the brink of financial ruin to be richer than I ever dreamed.

Who would have imagined that easy-to-follow instructions and simple ideas like the ones I chose to act on from Tom's monthly communications would do this: **in 4 short months I doubled my income!**
*Chris Bowman, Charlotte, NC*

Are the things I did work for you? Check out what dentists across the country and beyond are saying. So, if you're ready for success at warp speed, reach out and

help yourself to **five months worth of:**

## Gems Insiders' Circle Silver Membership FREE.
### NO RISK. NO CHARGE. NO STRINGS. NO HYPE.

You'll get a giant cache of gems, including three recent months of materials plus two months going forward, all for a one-time charge of $5.95 to cover postage.

Your **Fully Guaranteed**, trial membership includes:

- Three recent, strategy-crammed issues of my *Independent Dentist Newsletter* as soon as you sign up followed by an exciting new issue every month. This brainstorm-filled publication is THE resource for dentists who ready to get in on the action.

- Instant access to my *Million Dollar Resources Directory,* the place to find everything you need cheap -- or at least at the very best prices.

- Three of my most recent *"Mastermind of the Month"* CD series -- interviews with Masterminds like Dr. Gordon Christensen, Dr. Charles Blair, Mr. Greg Stanley, Dr. Ray Bertolotti and many others you may have not had the opportunity to hear. You'll also receive additional Mastermind CDs delivered monthly -- PLUS 15 AGD-PACE credits per year just for listening to (and profiting from) them.

- *Breakthrough thinking from the archives of Mr. Alan Thornberg,* practice transition specialist and all-around genius.

- *Five Silver Letter* inserts (three recent, two ongoing.) These monthly communications from the edge bristle with unorthodox, but highly effective ideas.

"Since we began receiving your gems, just 9 months ago, our collectible production is up **over $116,000 a year** and most of that increase is NET PROFIT!" -- Carter Gampp, DDS, Phoenix, AZ

### Are You Starting to See How Much This Could Mean to You?
Read on -- and keep in mind I'm just

scratching the surface of all you'll receive.

- *Three recent issues of my GoldMine Newsletter:* Lots of dentists consider this monthly publication absolutely essential to their success.

- Twice a year my Silver members receive a CD with studio quality photos of great new VIP patient gifts and information on where you can buy them wholesale -- often at savings of 40 - 60%. As a FREE TRIAL Member you'll receive one of these CDs, too, with JPEG images, you can drop them into ads, flyers, postcards -- whatever you need to impress entice and motivate your best patients.

- *Private e-mail access to me* through members' "Ask The Gems Guy"!

- The chance to sit in on live quarterly *teleconferences with my masterminds.*

"I have doubled my income in the last five months and have had time to take several weeks off."
-- *Ranvir Dhillon, DMD, Hounslow, England*

### Access Online 24/7 to Gems Proprietary Strategic Documents
Take a look at just some of what you'll find waiting for you:

- **"The Secret to How I Resigned From Delta But KEPT Most of My Delta Patients!"**

- **"Seven Magic Phrases Your Dental Receptionist Can Use Today** to Effortlessly Build an IRON CAGE Around Your Patients... Case 'Acceptance' is NOT 'Acceptance' until you INSURE Acceptance of Your Financial Arrangements."

- **"A Financial Options Form to Help Patients Say Yes While Making YOU a TON More Money"**

- **"VERBAL SKILLS that NAIL 87% Adult Acceptance of Fluoride"**

- "Discover the Secret to **Effortlessly & Instantly Boosting Your Average Cosmetic Case Acceptance**

# OFFER ENDS
# 10 DAYS FROM BOOK SHIP DATE

## FOR *FASTEST* ACTION FAX NOW TO 1-508-861-1550

❑ YES, <u>PLEASE SIGN ME UP</u>
**for the GIC FREE TRIAL SILVER MEMBERSHIP.**
I authorize you to bill my credit card $5.95 now and $79.50 per month
starting in Month 3. **I AM FREE TO CANCEL AT ANY TIME and
keep everything I've received.**

*For your protection, **<u>please include the 3-digit Security Code</u>** on the
back of your card.*

Doctor's Name _____

Address _____

City_____State_____Zip_____Country ____

Phone_____Fax _____

Email _____

**Credit Card:**
❑ MC     ❑ Visa  ❑ Amex     ❑ Disc     Expiration Date____/_____

Card # _____3-digit code _____

Exact Name on Card: _____

**Cardholder Signature:** _____

My signature here authorizes Dr. Tom Orent and Gems Publishing USA, Inc. to
charge the credit card listed for the amounts shown, and to use email, fax, phone and
mailing addresses to keep me informed of new products and special offers made
available from time to time.

**ECSBK-1**

**As You Can See, There's a Million Dollar Bill at the Top of This Page and There's More Where That Came From Because...**

# I'll Show You How to Discover the HIDDEN WEALTH in Your Dental Practice Absolutely FREE – if You ACT NOW!

Dear Friend,

No matter how hard you work you just can't seem to get ahead  -- or give your family the things dentists' families enjoyed when you were a kid.

You know why -- managed care, patients who refuse needed treatment, staff hassles -- all the things that leave you driving to work every day with stress as your passenger. Which is why it's so important that you read this letter, and learn how you can:

**Totally Obliterate the Things That Are Killing Your Practice and Trouble...Even Triple Your Income**

You know me. I'm Dr. Tom Orent. You've read my columns, maybe even bought my books or attended my seminars.

People call me "the Gems Guy" because my easy-to-implement practice and income-building ideas (GEMS!) have changed the lives of 16,543 dentists for the better.

"My life feels forever changed as we have been averaging almost an **extra $50,000** in production, above and beyond what was once normal'". -- Dr. Kory Wegner, Milwaukee, WI

My gems were born out of necessity. My practice had one foot in the grave and needed strategies that were quick and effective (not to mention cheap). And I discovered a ton of them, with result that in just three years I went from the brink of financial ruin to becoming richer than I ever dreamed.

Who would have imagined that easy-to-follow instructions and simple ideas like the ones I chose to act on from Tom's monthly communications would do this: **in 4 short months I doubled my income!**
-- Chris Bowman, Charlotte, NC

Did the things I did work for you? Check out what dentists across the country and beyond are saying. So, if you're ready for success at warp speed, reach out and

help yourself to **five months worth of:**

## Gems Insiders' Circle Silver Membership FREE.
### NO RISK. NO CHARGE. NO STRINGS. NO HYPE.

You'll get a giant cache of gems, including three recent months of materials plus two months going forward, all for a one-time charge of $5.95 to cover postage.

Your **Fully Guaranteed**, trial membership includes:

- Three recent, strategy-crammed issues of my *Independent Dentist Newsletter* as soon as you sign up followed by an exciting new issue every month. This brainstorm-filled publication is THE resource for dentists who ready to get in on the action.
- Instant access to my *Million Dollar Resources Directory,* the place to find everything you need cheap -- or at least at the very best prices.
- Three of my most recent *"Mastermind of the Month"* CD series -- interviews with Masterminds like Dr. Gordon Christensen, Dr. Charles Blair, Dr. Greg Stanley, Dr. Ray Bertolotti and many others you may have not had the opportunity to hear. You'll also receive additional Mastermind CDs delivered monthly -- PLUS 15 AGD-PACE credits per year just for listening to (and profiting from) them.
- *Breakthrough thinking from the archives of Mr. Alan Thornberg*, practice transition specialist and all-around genius.
- *Five Silver Letter* inserts (three recent, two ongoing.) These monthly communications from the edge bristle with unorthodox, but highly effective ideas.

"Since we began receiving your gems, just 9 months ago, our collectible production is up **over $116,000 a year** and most of that increase is NET PROFIT!"-- Carter Gampp, DDS, Phoenix, AZ

### Are You Starting to See How Much This Could Mean to You?
Read on -- and keep in mind I'm just

scratching the surface of all you'll receive.
- *Three recent issues of my GoldMine Newsletter:* Lots of dentists consider this monthly publication absolutely essential to their success.
- Twice a year my Silver members receive a CD with studio quality photos of great new VIP patient gifts and information on where you can buy them wholesale -- often at savings of 40 - 60%. As a FREE TRIAL Member you'll receive one of these CDs, too, with JPEG images, you can drop them into ads, flyers, postcards -- whatever you need to impress entice and motivate your best patients.
- *Private e-mail access to me* through members' "Ask The Gems Guy"!
- The chance to sit in on live quarterly *teleconferences with my masterminds.*

"I have **doubled my income** in the last five months and have had time to take several weeks off."
-- Ranvir Dhillon, DMD, Hounslow, England

### Access Online 24/7 to Gems Proprietary Strategic Documents
Take a look at just some of what you'll find waiting for you:

- **"The Secret to How I Resigned From Delta But KEPT Most of My Delta Patients!"**
- **"Seven Magic Phrases Your Dental Receptionist Can Use Today** to Effortlessly Build an IRON CAGE Around Your Patients... Case 'Acceptance' is NOT 'Acceptance' until you INSURE Acceptance of Your Financial Arrangements."
- **"A Financial Options Form to Help Patients Say Yes While Making YOU a TON More Money"**
- **"VERBAL SKILLS that NAIL 87% Adult Acceptance of Fluoride"**
- "Discover the Secret to **Effortlessly & Instantly Boosting Your Average Cosmetic Case Acceptance**

# OFFER ENDS
# 10 DAYS FROM BOOK SHIP DATE

## FOR *FASTEST* ACTION FAX NOW TO 1-508-861-1550

❑ **YES, <u>PLEASE SIGN ME UP</u>**
**for the GIC FREE TRIAL SILVER MEMBERSHIP.**
I authorize you to bill my credit card $5.95 now and $79.50 per month
starting in Month 3. **I AM FREE TO CANCEL AT ANY TIME and
keep everything I've received.**

*For your protection, <u>**please include the 3-digit Security Code**</u> on the
back of your card.*

Doctor's Name _____

Address_____

City_____State_____Zip_____Country _____

Phone_____Fax _____

Email _____

**Credit Card:**
❑ MC     ❑ Visa ❑ Amex     ❑ Disc     Expiration Date_____/_____

Card # _____3-digit code _____

Exact Name on Card: _____

**Cardholder Signature:** _____

My signature here authorizes Dr. Tom Orent and Gems Publishing USA, Inc. to
charge the credit card listed for the amounts shown, and to use email, fax, phone and
mailing addresses to keep me informed of new products and special offers made
available from time to time.

ECSBK-1